M000086509

Wake Up Beauty!

Wake Up Beauty!

IT'S NOT ABOUT THE PRINCE

Lisa Marie Jenkins

NEW YORK

Wake Up, Beauty!
IT'S NOT ABOUT THE PRINCE!

© 2014 Lisa Marie Jenkins.

All rights reserved. No portion of this book may be reproduced, stored in a retrieval system, or transmitted in any form or by any means—electronic, mechanical, photocopy, recording, scanning, or other,—except for brief quotations in critical reviews or articles, without the prior written permission of the publisher.

Published in New York, New York, by Morgan James Publishing. Morgan James and The Entrepreneurial Publisher are trademarks of Morgan James, LLC. www.MorganJamesPublishing.com

The Morgan James Speakers Group can bring authors to your live event. For more information or to book an event visit The Morgan James Speakers Group at www.TheMorganJamesSpeakersGroup.com.

A FREE eBook edition is available
with the purchase of this print book

CLEARLY PRINT YOUR NAME IN THE BOX ABOVE

Instructions to claim your free eBook edition:
1. Download the BitLit app for Android or iOS
2. Write your name in UPPER CASE in the box
3. Use the BitLit app to submit a photo
4. Download your eBook to any device

ISBN 978-1-63047-243-6 paperback
ISBN 978-1-63047-244-3 eBook
ISBN 978-1-63047-245-0 hardcover
Library of Congress Control Number:
2014937938

Cover Design by:
Rachel Lopez
www.r2cdesign.com

Interior Design by:
Bonnie Bushman
bonnie@caboodlegraphics.com

In an effort to support local communities, raise awareness and funds, Morgan James Publishing donates a percentage of all book sales for the life of each book to Habitat for Humanity Peninsula and Greater Williamsburg.

Get involved today, visit
www.MorganJamesBuilds.com

Habitat
for Humanity®
Peninsula and
Greater Williamsburg
Building Partner

Contents

Happily Ever After: The Myth and the Truth

Once upon a time there lived a young maiden named Snow White. She dreamed and hoped that one day she would finally find freedom and true love, to begin her life of *happily ever after*. Unfortunately, Snow White was a scullery maid, imprisoned in a life of unappreciated servitude and loveless isolation. She fell into this dreary existence after her father died and left her to the devices of a very angry, entitled queen—her stepmother. There was, however, one tiny possibility that Snow White could find love and happiness, but it required that she be discovered and rescued by a handsome and wealthy prince. Prince Charming was her only ray of hope to finding *happily ever after*. She wanted her prince so badly because she believed it would transform her into a gracious and regal queen....

STOP RIGHT THERE! Are you following this? The only way to become free, lovable, and live happily ever after as women is *if and only if* a man shows up to discover and rescue us. Without a man—a father or husband—women are destined either to be scullery maids or angry, entitled queens? The only way to become a regal and gracious queen is through the love of our Prince Charming? What about our power, our freedom, and our self-proclamation that love comes from within, that women are not only capable but responsible for creating their own happiness? These fairy tales don't represent *happily ever after*. They are dark tales of oppressed and powerless women. I invite you to join me on a journey to becoming the beautiful, regal, and gracious queen you were born to be!

As women, it is so easy to feel disempowered, unaware of the gracious and beautiful spirit that lies within each of us, just waiting to emerge. From the day we are born, we are taught and conditioned to believe that our nirvana or bliss will be found with that "special love," that romantic love, and one day we will find our holy grail when we find our Prince Charming. I have great news for you: you can find what you are looking for, and you have total control over creating your very own *happily ever after*, because it's not about the guy (or the girl), it's all about you! What you are truly seeking is the experience of falling in love, which at its essence, is the experience of passion, wholeness, and purpose. So here is the even better news: you don't have to rely on anyone or anything outside of you to experience these feelings of love. *Happily ever after* is available to you, with or without your Prince Charming. So stop waiting to be rescued or discovered and start living a life of love, bliss, and passion. You, Beauty, are the one you have been waiting for!

Our Outdated DNA

The feeling that we need to find a partner goes even deeper than what we were taught or what we absorbed from our mothers, marketing, and societal pressure. It is actually in our DNA from thousands of years ago. It's a lot like the way our fight or flight response works; when our fight or flight response gets triggered, ninety-nine percent of the time nothing is physically threatening to hurt us. Just the thought of a perceived threat automatically triggers a very physical response; our cortisol levels and adrenaline soar to help us physically fight or flee to escape. This physical response is hardwired within us. The same holds true for the deep, hardwired feelings within a woman that tell her, she is not okay or safe without a man. At one time, a woman needed a man for her survival. Her odds of living were much greater with the physical strength and hunting abilities of a man by her side. We still carry that primal force in our DNA today.

Those genes are still with us today, so it makes sense there is still a "find a man or die" mentality hardwired within us. Of course, I know in my own mind that I will not die if I don't have a partner—but I can honestly say I have experienced a level of fear so deep and primal, it felt like I was going to die. Like most women, my greatest pain and suffering was inherited from my mother's misconceptions about herself, which had been passed down through generations.

My mother was an attractive woman, with beautiful blue eyes, ivory skin, and dark hair. But underneath, there was still a much-wounded little girl believing she was not good enough or loveable.

She met and married my father, Edward Roy Steinmeyer, at age twenty-three. I believe my parents shared a very special bond. Even thirty years after my father passed, he remained the love of my mother's life. Their relationship was quite dysfunctional at times; they could get in an argument and not speak to each other for a week. My mother's emotional withdrawal, coupled with my father's inability to address conflict, made finding resolution a difficult task. The pain would eventually subside and they would act as if nothing had happened. The unresolved conflict was often buried under the rug with subconscious resentments waiting to be unleashed during the next misunderstanding or disagreement. But I know they were committed, loyal to one another, and shared great physical affection.

On Christmas Eve, 1971, when I was eight years old, I was laying on the floor watching television, with my father sitting behind me on the sofa. Our regular Christmas tradition was to attend the candlelight service at the United Church of Christ, but my father said his back was hurting too much to sit in the church pew. He had been complaining for a few months about back pain and had been x-rayed, but doctors had been unable to discover the cause. That evening, he suffered a massive heart attack and began gasping for air. He urgently told me to get my mom.

My father was a police officer and a medal of valor recipient for the city of St. Louis—when a cop was in trouble, everyone showed up. So what I remember most about that night were the many police cars and the ambulance parked in our cul-de-sac. My mother jumped in the back of the ambulance with my father without a second thought about me. A neighbor I barely knew whisked me off to their home. My father was put in intensive care and moved about a week later to a regular room.

A few nights after leaving intensive care, my father had late evening visitors. It was January 2, 1972. My mother had been at the hospital that evening, but a snowstorm was moving in and my father urged her to head home before the roads became hazardous. That evening, with a sparkle in her eye, my mom told me she knew he was feeling better because he gave her a little slap on the bottom as she walked away from his bed. At this point, everyone assumed he was out of the woods and would be returning home soon.

After my mother's departure from the hospital that evening, two police officers and their wives stopped by unexpectedly to see my father. That night he experienced another massive heart attack, which ultimately took his life. The nurse on duty said he must have been experiencing the heart attack while the visitors were still there, as the door had not even closed behind them when my dad hit the help button for the nurse's station. My father was too proud to tell them he wasn't feeling well and ask them to leave—so much so that it probably cost him his life the next day. To him, saying he needed help would have shown weakness as a man. After my dad's death and as long as I can remember, my mother would call me her "blessing in disguise." As an adult, my Mom explained to me that she was suicidal for quite a while after my father's death. She said if she hadn't had me to raise, she truly would have given up and taken her own life. This is what made me a blessing, since I became her reason and purpose to go on with life. The blessing was in disguise, however, because I was an unexpected pregnancy that happened ten years after her last child at the age of thirty-nine—a very late age to have children in the 1960s.

In the months following my dad's passing, she often stayed in her bedroom for days, crying. I can remember, at eight years old, feeling so completely alone and abandoned—my father was suddenly gone, and now my mother was emotionally gone.

My mother once said that one day I came home from school and cried inconsolably for a very long period of time. When she was finally able to get me to tell her what was wrong, I responded, "We are not as good as other people, because we don't have a daddy." I am sure this serious misbelief came from my mom's behavior and also from knowing there were really no other kids in my classroom or neighborhood without a father.

My mother didn't believe she was good enough without my father, and this type of belief can be absorbed by children almost through osmosis. I carried this belief and feeling with me, subconsciously, well into adulthood. The simple belief that I was not as good as other people without a father evolved into my belief, as an adult, that I was not as good as other people without a boyfriend, partner, or husband. Ultimately this belief led me home, down the path to the truth of who I am—as you'll see later.

A year or so after my father's death, my mother became very interested in metaphysics and was enjoying the company of several close girlfriends. She seemed to be doing really well and enjoying life again. For many years, there were Edgar Cayce study groups, Spiritual Frontiers meetings, and past-life hypnosis sessions going on in our home weekly. This might not sound so peculiar, until you realize it was the 1970s! Then my mom met Darrell Stansberry and married him when I was eleven. My siblings and I called him "Dur'll." He was the same age as my mother and had just retired from the Air Force as a Lt. Colonel, but seemed to have a chip on his shoulder that he had not made full bird. He was very recently divorced with five children, lived in a trailer, was a functional alcoholic, and was flat broke. For the most part, only his two youngest children even spoke to him. Darrell was not a best stepfather pick under any circumstances. Even at age eleven, I knew I did not want her to marry him. I even shared my feelings with my adult neighbor and babysitter, who corrected me and told me I was being selfish, that I should be happy for my mom, because she would no longer be alone.

Well, Darrell cheated on my mom. Her health deteriorated over the years with him due to her constantly distraught emotional state. They split at one point, but then reconciled after a few months. My mom was in agony at the thought of being alone again, even though at that point she was capable of supporting herself financially and her relationship was causing her so much pain. She stayed married to him for thirteen years and finally divorced immediately after my college graduation.

I have so much compassion for my mom now, after going through my own darkness and experiencing my own desperate feelings that I needed a man to be okay. For all the pain I suffered and put myself through, I can only imagine the even greater magnitude of desperation she must have felt to have stayed with Darrell. Sadly, my mother never fully got to realize that she was not a victim and that she was already whole and perfect, with or without a man. She died at age seventy-eight.

My mom brought me up to believe feelings were just feelings, and they could not be changed or controlled. But I also was told to control my emotions or they would control me. Looking back now, this sounds like a recipe for emotional prison. This belief came from a woman who had experienced severe abuse as a child, then experienced amazing healing and gained huge metaphysical knowledge, and came to understand universal and spiritual law. Unfortunately, she never made the connection that beliefs create our thoughts, and thoughts create our feelings, and emotions are only the final manifestations.

So most of my relationship trauma stemmed from this one simple error in belief, which I inherited from my mother and adopted as my subconscious truth: *I needed a man, a romantic relationship, to be whole and happy.* This belief left me helpless and at the mercy of whatever man was in my life. However, my work life was quite different. My mantra at work was "fake it till you make it"—the more insecure I felt, the more I would "act as if" I had it all and knew what I was doing. This mindset led me to a six-figure salary in a technology field, with only a bachelor's degree in physical education.

But as successful as I was in my career, it didn't change the fact that I felt utterly dependent on a romantic relationship for my self-worth. It wasn't until I was in my forties, when I discovered I could control or change my thoughts, that my thoughts had been the manifestation for everything in my life. It was the biggest lightbulb moment of my life! Until that point, I was a victim of wherever my random and habitual thoughts took me. I lived in a purely reactionary state, was a servant to my thoughts, and allowed life to just happen to me. Imagine teaching children how their relationship to thought creates their life experience. The ability to uncover subconscious misbeliefs behind negative thought patterns could alleviate so much human suffering.

Believing I had no control over my feelings was responsible for most of my own personal suffering, which was focused on romantic relationships and the men in my life. This, combined with the conditioning from my mother that she was not good enough without a man, set me up for a painful journey that ultimately led to thousands of hours of contemplation, analyzing, and a desperate desire to get out of pain. Don't get me wrong—I don't blame my mother. Without this experience, I would never have been so driven to find peace, love, and wholeness in my life. I have only immense compassion for my mother now—no resentment, no blame, only true gratitude for her experience and mine, which gave me the opportunity to heal the legacy.

In fact, my journey to finally realizing that *I am good enough without a man* has been the most liberating experience of my life. This is the journey to wholeness. This is what women need to understand to truly flourish and love life, no matter what or who is in our life. Most importantly, this is what will free us to live a life of purpose and to serve our calling with passion.

I remember reading a story about a world-renowned therapist who was asked to volunteer with Cambodian refugees in American immigration camps. These people had endured immense suffering. Their journeys in the cargo holds of ships to America were plagued with starvation, illness, death, and dysentery. Many parents lost young children during the trip itself, then they were placed in camps and separated from loved ones with no freedom in sight. The therapist felt humbled by the request and wondered what she could possibly offer to anyone that had experienced such hardships in life. She was astonished to find that what people wanted to talk about was the heartache they experienced from loss of romantic love. For example, one woman shared her devastation about her lover leaving her for another woman and was consumed with how to get him back, even more than everything else she had experienced.

To me, this demonstrates the magnitude of significance we put on romantic relationships as our source of happiness and wholeness. This human conditioning knows no bounds, yet it can be our greatest call to WAKE UP!

You Are a Cupcake

Imagine a cupcake, moist and sweet, thick with frosting. Now, a cupcake is yummy, whole, and complete all by itself, but adding sprinkles could make it even better, right? Think of yourself as a cupcake. Just as you don't need sprinkles to truly enjoy a cupcake, you don't need a romantic partner to enjoy a passionate and complete life—but a partner can certainly make it better. A partner is the festive sprinkles on top that can only augment your already whole and fulfilling life. The key is to upgrade your desire for a partner from a need to a preference. You don't *need* a partner to be complete and happy, but you may *prefer* to have a partner to share life with. It's sort of like saying you would prefer to have sushi for dinner tonight, but steak is okay, too. Turning a preference into a need immediately releases attachment to needing something outside of you in order to be okay. It is universal law that, when we feel we must have something specific in our life to be happy or fulfilled—in other words, if we are *attached* to having to have it—we actually keep it away; it sets up an energetic block. But, release the attachment to having to have it and POOF—there it is! It is sort of like holding a handful of sand. You can hold a lot of sand with a gentle and open hand, but clench your fist to hold on tight and you end up with an empty hand.

I am not saying in any way that a loving and soulful relationship isn't totally possible and desirable—of course it is, and most of us want and deserve it. I am only saying that another person can't complete you. It requires two whole people gently coming together to create a deep, loving relationship, each person knowing they are responsible for their own happiness and growth with no expectations that the other is responsible for making them feel happy or complete. That is a ridiculously tall order to expect from anyone, not to mention impossible for another to provide. It is unfair and unrealistic to cling to that idea. We have all seen that kind of codependent relationship, though. It is especially common from my parents' generation. The man often became the rock for the woman and she had no idea who she was or how to rely on herself in any way without a husband. To me, that is tragic and often why when one partner dies, the other goes shortly thereafter. There is no sense of self without the constant re-validation from a partner. Some people may see that as true love and I suppose there is a certain sweetness about it, but I don't believe deep fulfillment and meaning can exist with such imbalance. Not knowing who I am without another person sounds terrifying to me. I have experienced it, and it feels desperate and needy. It is a dysfunctional entanglement, not true unconditional love, when you can't tell where one person stops and the other person starts.

Remember that line in *Jerry Maguire* when Tom Cruise says, "You complete me," and everyone melts? I say, bullshit! That is more of the stuff we buy into that keeps us looking outside ourselves for wholeness and happiness, which is a bottomless pit, a never-ending search. When you take full responsibility for your passion and wholeness, the deep-rooted attachment to finding a loving partner falls away, and you then create space either for a healthy potential partner to show up, or to deepen and grow your existing relationship. In essence, you are saying, "I love me first, and then you." Most of society would call that selfish, when in fact it is the opposite. Let go of attachment to something, and the door swings wide open for it to show up! It's like the couple trying everything to get pregnant, and the minute they adopt, she gets pregnant. I know a girlfriend that wanted so badly to get married, and it just wasn't happening, no matter how hard she searched for a husband. She finally decided she would marry herself and that she was the most important person in her life. She went out and bought a beautiful diamond engagement ring. Yep, you guessed it: the man she ended up marrying showed up right after this bold purchase.

When we wait to be discovered, to be rescued, to be kissed by a prince in hopes that we will feel our soul emerge and experience bliss and our *happily ever after*, we give up our power and the ability to make it happen from within ourselves. Here is the honest truth: *You, Beauty, are the one you have been waiting for!*

Think about it. You are the one constant in your life. You will be with you from birth to death, so isn't it logical that you are responsible for your own *happily ever after?* You start by learning to love your own company and becoming your own best friend. Besides, what happens if you meet the love of your life, your Prince Charming, and he dies? Does that mean your chance at a happily-ever-after life is doomed? I sure hope not.

I recently met a woman whose second husband truly was the love of her life. She described their love as peaceful and deep. They were best friends. Three years into the relationship, with both careers flourishing, while building the house of their dreams on the water in Florida, he abruptly had a heart attack and died. Of course it was sad and required grieving, but it didn't have to be tragic. It didn't mean her life was over and she would never feel joy and love again. In her case, it wasn't over at all. She grew as a person and learned to move on and love life again, because she valued and loved herself. Several years later, she did meet another great man and is now engaged. She is experiencing romantic love again, but she is beautiful and whole with or without him and she knows it, which is exactly why Prince Charming keeps showing up in her life—she doesn't need him around to be happy.

The Prince's Kiss

Brace yourself, because I am about to tell you the true story of Snow White, the one that no one ever told you. Be warned though, this revelation might invoke the same feeling you had when you found out the Easter Bunny and Santa Claus didn't really exist. Here it is: Snow White *did not wake up* when Prince Charming kissed her; she actually *went to sleep.* It's true! She went to sleep on herself. Her dreams. Her passions. She believed that romantic love meant she no longer had to ignite her own passion and emerge from her truth and find purpose in life. She stopped taking responsibility for her own happiness and fulfillment. Sleeping Beauty and *all* the princesses believed that romantic love was meant to provide happiness to her, so she stalled her own journey of enlightenment, her own evolution as a spiritual being.

Romantic *love* is a fantasy. Romance is not love. It is lust, infatuation, and it always wears off. That is one reason people become relationship or love addicts and keep searching, attempting to find the one where the lust never fades. Oftentimes we are programmed to believe romance should always continue, but searching for that fantasy will only cause pain. A marriage is not one long date. The romance will fade away. Ongoing infatuation is an illusion we buy into from romance novels, fairy tales, and societal conditioning. It is the belief that finding the right partner and having the perfect wedding will bring us joy.

Now please, don't take this the wrong way. This in no way means that romantic relationships can't move into a deeper and fulfilling love after the disillusionment and disappointment subside. In fact, that evolution is the true purpose of this special relationship. We often have an illusion of who we believe someone is, who we want them to be to make ourselves feel great, and we project parts of ourselves onto that person. In other words, we don't see the person as who they actually are, but instead we see them with a sort of positive prejudice. We project characteristics on them that resolve our own vulnerabilities or shortcomings. We are attracted to what we need, our complement. When we start to feel romantic attraction, it is a signal that we are attempting to mold that person into someone we want them to be in order to fulfill our own needs.

But when we begin to see the person in reality, problems start. We think, "They are not who I thought they would be. They are responsible for my unhappiness, and I am not getting what I want from them." The reason the honeymoon period of a relationship, usually the first three months, is so blissful and exciting is because the two halves do make a whole, reminding us how we are meant to feel when we alone are whole and complete. As we all know, this doesn't last. When it fades, the real work begins. This is the pivotal point when we can choose to wake up. Romantic love is a calling to do our own work, not for the other person to fulfill and complete us. We have the opportunity to love, nurture, and cultivate in ourselves what we thought we saw in the other person. When we realize the romantic relationship can be a vehicle to find our way home, to our own truth and joy, the relationship can then transition into a deeper, more meaningful stage. This is when the romantic relationship can become a holy relationship—after all, isn't that what it is meant to be—holy matrimony?

The Holy Relationship

The holy relationship happens when both people accept that the relationship has a purpose and foundation in each person's spiritual growth, individual evolution, or enlightenment. There is nothing like a romantic relationship to shed light on the dark places within us that still need healing. Why else do you think relationships can be full of turmoil, hurt, big reactions, and emotion? The other person serves as a mirror to show us our shadow side or undesirable traits and brings up our wounds and insecurities like in no other relationship. These areas need light shined on them so we can see the unloving or unkind aspects of ourselves. It's guaranteed—if there is an attraction, there is the ability to grow and heal from that relationship, whether it is short-term or life-long.

Here's the good news/bad news. The good news is that the romantic relationship can provide a vehicle for us to become more enlightened, if we are willing to take a look at ourselves, own what we see, and evolve from the mirror image our partner presents to us. Both people have to be committed to the relationship and willing to take a look at themself instead of pointing fingers at the other. A perfect example of misplaced blame is when one person says to the other, "You make me feel, you make me behave this way…" The holy relationship serves as a conduit for each individual to find a path to their own enlightenment. Courage and commitment are necessary, as are the willingness to be wrong and the ability to say, "Thank you for showing me the wounded places within me that are not of love or light. I will take a look at that and heal those not-so-pretty or unkind places within me."

The bad news is that our society has become accustomed to pointing fingers at another when our weaknesses start showing up. We avoid looking at our own shortcomings and will do anything to be right. Our behavior is driven by the need for external validation and to protect ourselves at all cost, so no one really sees the true person underneath, our self-disdain or vulnerability. Yet having the courage to look in the mirror and be truly vulnerable is the way to healing and liberation. Allowing ourselves to be vulnerable is the only way to ever be totally safe. When we stand in our truth, there is nothing to hide. And the truth is that you can't shut down or hide the dark parts of yourself without snuffing out your light too.

Let that sink in fully. You can't be selective. According to research from bestselling author Brené Brown, when you disconnect from part of your truth, you're disconnecting from your whole truth—the good and the bad.[1] Until we allow our authenticity to be fully exposed, our behaviors will continue to be an expression of the wounded child, the lack of self-love, within each of us. And the greater the need for healing, the greater the call for love, and the worse the behavior. An extreme example would be a child who has been abandoned and abused, has lived in foster homes, and has never felt love or acceptance. Often times this child will do horrific things to prospective adoptive parents. But in fact, the child's behavior is a cry for love and a defense mechanism to avoid feeling any more rejection. They subconsciously keep love away in fear of feeling rejected and unloved. As this person becomes an adult, they continually play this dynamic out in relationships—desperately wanting to feel love, while simultaneously behaving in ways that pushes love away. So although it's misguided, all negative and dysfunctional behavior is just a call for love.

We have to peel back the layers of armor we have created so that we can heal. Most of this protection consists of defense mechanisms we created to survive as children, but carrying them into our adult relationships only creates dysfunction and inhibits true intimacy. And that's where the blame game begins—unless we've made a commitment to use the relationship as a path to enlightenment. Eventually, if enough hurt and resentment have been created, this can create a canyon of divide and lead to a point where two people can't get back to the feeling of love they once held for each other. Does this sound familiar?

Romance is guaranteed to die, but true love can happen if you are willing to do your work. Healing yourself through your romantic relationship helps heal the world. Being in love with who you are at the deepest level is what *happily ever after* truly means. It means falling in love with *you*!

Just Turn on the Light

Several years ago I worked with a medical intuitive named MaryAnne. She was a registered nurse, but she could energetically and intuitively sense the dis-ease in someone's physical body, the emotional imbalance being created, and the best way to help support the physical to get back in harmony on all levels. She was powerful, yet lovely and peaceful. She was no doubt an angel in my life. In fact, she was like a fairy godmother, helping me see my own power by showing me that I went to sleep on myself whenever I fell in love. MaryAnne led me to my own awakening story.

In the movie, I love it when Cinderella exclaims, "Oh, Fairy Godmother, I thought you'd never get here!" The Fairy Godmother responds, "Oh, that's not true, or I couldn't have come." How metaphysical is that? It means we can't create anything we don't think and believe in. Then there is Glenda, the Good Witch from *The Wizard of Oz*, who told Dorothy, "You have always had the power to go home, but you had to learn it for yourself." I love it when deep spiritual meaning is revealed in fairy tales. But it's easy to miss when we read them from the wrong perspective—the Prince Charming perspective.

Even today, in a modern society and a free country, so many women don't realize the power and beauty they have within them—even highly successful women at the top of their career and who appear to have it all together. Even they may continue to seek after their Prince as their savior, and as a result are plagued by devastating romantic experiences over and over. I know this path well.

Sometimes we need the help of a fairy godmother or guide to help us discover our own power within. We each have a unique purpose in life and are meant to share it with the world to help evolve the human race and save the planet. Our divine plan is like a permanent computer program, stored in the cloud, and can never be deleted. It is our blueprint for joy and purpose. It's already inside us—we don't have to go out to find it. We just have to reveal it—let go of all the stuff that's blocking our view of it, like a cloud covering the sun. Just because you can't see the sun doesn't mean it isn't there.

We all have a story, we all have wounds, and whatever makes us uniquely different is what will ultimately reveal our path to wholeness, and it is the difference we can make in the world with our unique message of gift. Our message is our life art; it can be anything that contributes to helping the human race and relieve suffering. The truth is that we have a responsibility to heal ourselves from the inside out, not just for ourselves, but to model this wholeness as women for the world.

The journey toward finding true love that lasts forever is dependent on one factor: *you, Beauty!* So as you work your way through this book, you will discover how we as women fell asleep on ourselves in the first place. You'll discover your beautiful inner self—the Feminista. And you'll learn about the importance of living your life in truth and with passion. In Part Two, you will begin a journey of self-healing, casting away all past struggles and worries through a process of vulnerability, self-compassion, and inner wisdom. Your native genius will emerge, and your true gifts will begin to be unleashed. When you wake up to the truth of who you are, and live according to your native genius, your true feminine leadership will inspire others and create the change our world desperately needs.

In short, this book will welcome you home to your true nature of joy. It's already within you, and it's as unique as your fingerprint. It comes from your own spirit and true essence, and it is everlasting. So call off the search outside yourself and get ready to embark on the deep journey of discovery within.

Part One:

How Did We Fall Asleep on Ourselves?

One of my greatest strengths in the business world was my natural talent to lean in and speak up. When I felt inadequate, I would naturally tell myself to puff up and fake it until I made it. A sort of *act as if.* When I felt challenged or intimidated, I would lift my head and move forward with an attitude of confidence, even when it wasn't what I was feeling inside. Eventually, I wasn't acting at all; that regal, gracious queen I had been pretending to be in the professional world became who I truly was at my core. In fact, it was who I was always meant to be. We all have the ability to *act as if;* it's learning to adopt the feelings and thoughts *as if* the desired result has already occurred. When we align energetically to what we want to create, we naturally attract it. My courage to speak up and be heard, along with going for what I wanted, is directly related to my success in the corporate and financial world.

Yet in the context of romantic relationships, feeling inadequate left me in a pool of suffering, powerlessness, and emotional abuse. Rather than a gracious queen, I was a scullery maid, bound in servitude by my own feelings of unworthiness of love. My belief that I wasn't good enough as I truly was became both my greatest strength (professionally) and my greatest weakness (romantically). Professionally, the more insecure I felt, the more I took a courageous and driven position to overcome my feelings of inadequacy. Yet, in romantic relationships, I did the opposite; I didn't lean forward and speak up, because I knew that would end the relationship. Because I was tied to the belief that I needed a man to survive, I was not willing to risk losing the relationship, even at my own emotional expense, which came from deep fear of being abandoned and the intense painful feelings that would trigger for me. Yet both scenarios were rooted in my insecurity.

However, there was a significant difference: I was not *attached* to being successful in my career in the same way I was attached to having a relationship with a man. I believe that this nonattachment is what helped me succeed. I didn't see my success as validation of my self-worth and I didn't have to have professional success to be okay with me. I put on a suit of "I am good enough to be here, to do this, to make it," and before I realized it, I was exactly that. In contrast, I was very attached to finding a partner and keeping a partner, even when it wasn't a desirable relationship. I know this is deep, and quite frankly, it was mind boggling to me for years. Only when I healed the wounded girl who believed she needed a man was I truly able to understand. I now have a beautiful bridge of understanding that I believe I am meant to share with others: the bridge between success in the corporate professional world and the journey of spiritual enlightenment that ultimately will empower women in *all* areas.

For women, I believe it is a struggle to lean in and speak up in many areas of their life. Through the years, I have realized that it is for two core reasons: 1) they feel that have to speak up in a very masculine way in order to compete, which is neither intuitive nor comfortable, so they often just don't engage at all, or 2) they prioritize keeping peace and being liked over being heard, which results in sacrificing their own worth because they are not sharing their authentic self and gifts with others.

The following chapters will explore a woman's worth, our lineage, and why it is so critical that we start stepping up to invoke the feminine. This is not about equality; it is about balance. As women learn to lean in and be authentic by invoking the divine feminine, or sharing the goddess within each of us, men are then freed up to be authentic as well. The world has never needed more compassion, empathy, nurturing, and love than now. As women take their place as regal and gracious queens, as Beauties, our men will truly learn to be our kings.

Chapter 1

The Feminista:
Responsibility and Opportunity

 hat if I were to tell you that before your birth, angels descended upon you with the following message?

You are being born into a very important and transitional time on the planet. We are bestowing upon you both the opportunity and responsibility to help create a tidal wave of change to drive evolution. The planet has been ruled by masculine power for thousands of years, and it is now vital for you to help create balance and harmony by invoking the feminine power. Creating balance between the masculine and feminine energy, or

5

the yin and yang, is now necessary to evolve the human species to the next level and to sustain the planet.

Because you are being born during this pivotal and vital time when great healing to the earth is needed, it is important that you discover your passion and purpose, your life art, to fulfill your role. You are coming into the world with a very specific and personal destiny to contribute to this great change. You have a job to do, a calling to fulfill, a self to become. Your unique gift and contribution is a message the world will need.

If you are reading this book, then I know you were meant to hear this message and to be reminded of the commitment you made for your lifetime. The dominance of masculine power was necessary and got us where we are today, but now that we are ready to move to another level as a society, fully incorporating feminine power is vital to our survival.

Creating balance between masculine and feminine energy doesn't mean you have to be a feminist, and it doesn't mean you have to be angry or demand your fair share. Feminists have typically been focused on creating balance only for women, typically at the expense of men.

But the fact is that when women freely live out of their feminine power, it's good for men as well as women. It frees men from the pressure of having to make you happy, and it frees them to be themselves too, so you can both lead together. I met a young man on a recent plane trip who said, "When my wife is fully herself and balanced, I am in awe of her power and what she can do."

Rather than using outdated and self-centered term *feminist*, I'll use the term *Feminista*! A Feminista is about creating balance in the world for both men and women with joy. A Feminista is about consciousness, beauty, sensuality, and bonding together in sisterhood to create a tidal wave of change. She is here to emerge and align with her purpose, to live the truth of who she is. As you claim your power as a Feminista, you are igniting your native genius, your very unique blueprint, meant to be shared with the world. Being a Feminista means living from your whole heart, so that you may lead by example, pave the way, and leave a legacy. No matter how small or large your contribution may be, it is in you, just waiting for permission to be ignited. The same principle applies to our professional and corporate lives as well. To succeed in the future, the bottom-line profit of a company, power, and competing can no longer be the sole metrics of success, particularly when it comes at the expense of the sustainability of the planet. True success, in business as well as life, means everyone wins. Contributing to the greater good of humanity must be a component of every bottom line.

Emerge the Feminista

Where can you find your inner Feminista? It is in whatever you are resisting, it is in what you fear, it is where you play small, it is what has caused you the most pain. It's where you flow, and it's your personal assignment in the world. You bring it out by being still, tuning in, developing courage, living from the heart, and taking risks. You begin to know in your core that true success is so much greater than any failure you could experience along the way. Failure is how you will get there; it is part of the creative process. Failure coupled with persistence is what allows your vision to evolve and come into fruition. You can't teach anyone anything that you haven't struggled and persevered through yourself. In fact, failure along the way is necessary, so you may open to your soul's new direction, beyond thinking.

Masculine and Feminine Power Is Not
the Same as Male and Female

In October 2013, I conducted a workshop and participated in a panel discussion at the Xerox Women's Alliance Conference in New York. During the discussion, I made a statement about masculine power vs. feminine power and received the following survey comment from someone in the audience: "There were two technical women from STEM fields on the panel. It's unfortunate that this perspective was missing. 'Men got us technology and bridges'—WOW, what a sexist comment in a panel that's supposed to support women. This is part of the problem we have supporting girls in STEM."

This comment made me realize how much education is needed around masculine vs. feminine power. Let me be very clear: when we talk about the energetic balance between masculine and feminine energy, we are not talking about genders per se. Both genders have masculine and feminine energy; a balance between both is necessary for wholeness for each of us. The old gender roles where men are purely masculine and women are purely feminine no longer serve our species. We are in a state of flux, where roles are being redefined and both genders seek more balance within. Think of a pendulum swinging. It goes from one extreme to the other, slowly seeking balance—and always returns to the middle. The pendulum always has to swing to the other side before it can begin to find the center. It is now time for the pendulum to swing to the feminine power, to counter the extreme masculine power that has dominated for most of our known history.

The masculine power got us where we are today (hence bridges and technology), and it was needed. But in order for our species to evolve to the next level, the feminine power is required. In fact, our survival depends on it. Right now, we are killing our species and planet with the dominant masculine power. Think of it this way: all the plants and animals on the planet would be just fine if humans disappeared—in fact, they would be better off. But if all the plants and animals disappeared, humans could not survive. The planet needs love, respect, and nurturing to sustain our species, now more than ever. Nurturing *Mother* Earth and our species will take place through the feminine power, not the masculine.

Again, this is not a gender thing. There are certainly women who have a stronger masculine power than feminine, and vice versa. Up until a few years ago, I would say that my masculine was stronger than my feminine, which means I was not well balanced. It doesn't mean I wasn't feminine in my demeanor, dress, or sexual orientation. It means I stepped out, spoke up, and competed, and took action quickly, but without being directed from my creative and intuitive side—the feminine. This was a natural ability for me and I never thought much of it—until I noticed how many people commented on how unique it was for a woman to quickly make decisions and then act on those choices. Masculine means linear, analytical, clear, concise, competitive, and action oriented. It is one of the main reasons I did well in technology, a predominantly male industry. I worked well with men because I could speak their language when it came to business; I could lean forward, speak up, and clearly articulate with confidence what I wanted and needed.

Today, the majority of men still have more masculine than feminine attributes, energetically speaking. Heterosexual males often lack the feminine traits of being creative, intuitive, compassionate, empathetic, and collaborative. Most women in our society are still predominantly feminine and have trouble taking action and speaking up for themselves, even when they want to be heard. This is one of the main reasons that women are still the minority in leadership roles, even though we earn more degrees and start more businesses than men.

The masculine energy has ruled civilization for thousands of years. But while men can clearly be analytical and take action fearlessly, many aren't necessarily tuned into leading from a place of compassion, service, empathy, community, or intuition—in other words, it is not *inspired action*. Many women own these very loving and caring heartfelt feminine attributes, but lack the ability to make decisions and take action on what their heart says is true. Every being needs this balance. Since the feminine power in the world is lacking, women need to step up and ignite change to bring us back to a state of harmony. The bottom-line profit of a company, power, and competition can no longer be the sole focus when it comes at the expense of the sustainability of the planet. True success means everyone wins. Both men and women that are already tuned into creativity, intuition, heart, and compassion need to start taking action now and become empowered from their truth. The masculine power, which is great and was required to get us to this point in evolution, now needs to come from a deeper, more meaningful and nurturing place. Peace, love, unity, and respect are the higher goal.

Many men are still behind when it comes to emotional intelligence. There is both a physiological and societal reason for this. Physiologically, the corpus callosum (which connects the left and right brain) is much smaller in diameter within a man than a woman. This channel allows information received through the left brain to be processed in the right brain. For example, let's say a couple went to a counseling session together. Most women would be able to process whatever was being discussed intellectually and emotionally in real time, while the man would most likely need a few days to fully process emotionally. He would need his cave time. So, men literally have a bandwidth problem compared to women. This is also why men are generally great at work or activities that require hyper-tunnel vision or focus, and why women are usually much better taskmasters or multi-taskers.

The second reason men struggle with emotional intelligence is that men are usually not offered much practice when it comes to processing feelings and emotions. Men have been brought up in their *own* fairy tale, which says that a great man is a strong man, and it would be a sign of weakness to express feelings, especially tender or sad emotions. They don't know how to ask for help, and if they did, it would be considered a sign of weakness. Instead they have been taught that when faced with emotionally trying times to "man up" or "big boys don't cry." This creates a compartmentalized man who is competitive and disconnected from feelings and emotions. The modern man has been raised to be a warrior, without a connection to his heart.

I could not be more supportive of women in technology and science, because they are perfectly poised to help lead this needed shift in the world. Naturally balanced between the masculine and the feminine, they have the ability to both take action from a linear and analytical perspective (the masculine power) and be intuitive and compassionate (the feminine power). Add courage to that mix, and we have the perfect storm for evolving the world to the next level.

A Woman's Strengths

"The world will be saved by the Western woman."
—**Dalai Lama**, Vancouver Peace Summit, 2009

Why Western women? Because we are already privileged and empowered, but we still need to fully claim it! We have to take a front seat, stand in our power, be willing to be heard over being liked or pleasing others first. We have to learn to feel the fear and saddle up anyway in order to bring forth our true nature, our deepest calling.

> *During the women's suffrage movement, Alice Paul, one of the leaders of women's suffrage, staged a hunger strike while imprisoned for promoting women's right to vote, and was subsequently tied in a strait jacket and force-fed raw eggs until she vomited blood. Prison officials moved her to a sanitarium and they had a psychiatrist evaluate her in the hopes he would declare her insane. After his examination, the psychiatrist was asked if Alice's behavior indicated insanity. His reply? "Courage in women is often mistaken for insanity."*
> From Herstory Network, www.herstorynetwork.com/herstory-lessons/alice-paul

Does this need any more explanation? Women have been oppressed, raped, beaten, mutilated, and forced into prostitution and slavery for centuries. There can only be one reason men have tried to keep women suppressed: Women are powerful beyond belief!

Women have only had the right to vote in the United States since 1920, almost one hundred years. Many women dedicated their lives to this movement to ensure equality for women. Not only do we owe immense gratitude to these pioneers that paved the way for us, we have the responsibility to pick up the pace and continue the journey. If you haven't seen the movie *Iron Jawed Angels* with Hilary Swank portraying Alice Paul, I highly recommend you get the movie and have a screening with your friends. It will leave you overwhelmed with gratitude and hopefully also will inspire you to continue this movement and support other women to stand in their power. The next evolution of history needs to happen now and I believe it starts with women. Why continue to be prisoners of the past when we can be pioneers of the future? It is never the masses that create evolution; it usually begins with a small group of what are considered radical thinkers for their time.

After we moved through the crazy bra-burning women's lib movement of the 1970s, by the mid-1980s women reached a pivotal moment: We now earned fifty percent of all college degrees. Today, women earn sixty-five percent of all bachelor and graduate degrees. Still, as you can see from the current statistics for women in leadership (below), we are clearly a long way from holding fifty percent of leadership roles. Overall, women hold an average of only fifteen percent of leadership positions. More specifically, based on a report from Colorado Women's College, those percentages are:[2]

- 14% executives
- 17% board seats
- 18% elected officials
- 7.5% top earners

I hope these statistics shock you! At the current trajectory, it will take three centuries for women to reach parity with men. The world doesn't have three centuries. It is time to evolve and bring forward our feminine energy.

Women Can Bring It!

Catalyst, a research organization, found that companies with the most women board directors earned a 26 percent higher return on invested capital than companies with the least women.[3] McKinsey & Co. consulting firm found that international companies with more women on their corporate boards far outperformed the average company in return on equity and other measures. Operating profit was 56 percent higher. Overall research suggests that companies are more successful when they promote more women to senior jobs. It is about broadening the type of talent and therefore balancing the masculine and feminine in the world. Yet of Fortune 500 companies, roughly 18 percent of board members are female.[4] We need diversity.

The chart below shows that eight out of ten competencies desired for modern leaders are viewed as feminine traits, according to consultant John Gerzema, who was quoted in the *Harvard Business Review*.[5] This validates that the world needs us. We have already mastered these characteristics; now it is only a matter of putting them into action.

Viewed as Feminine	Viewed as Masculine
Expressive (#1)	Decisive (#3)
Plans for future (#2)	Resilient (#8)
Reasonable (#4)	
Loyal (#5)	
Flexible (#6)	
Patient (#7)	
Intuitive (#9)	
Collaborative (#10)	

Source: John Gerzema, BAV Consulting, WPP Group PLC

Insead Global Leadership Centre's study of the Top 10 Critical Components of Global Leadership revealed a different list of ten characteristics:[6]

1. Energizing
2. Designing & Aligning
3. Rewarding & Feedback
4. Team Building
5. Outside Orientation
6. Tenacity
7. Emotional Intelligence
8. Empowering
9. Global Mindset
10. Envisioning

Women scored above men on components 1 through 7. Women and men scored equally on components 8 and 9, and men outscored women only on only one component: envisioning. That means envisioning is the only component women need to develop to dominate global leadership strengths. Many believe that someone is either innately a visionary or not. I say it is a skill we can all learn. So let's start learning it right now! Up until now, we have been too busy trying to prove our competence rather than creating and selling our vision.

If envisioning is a skill we can learn, and it's critical we start now. All we need to do is open ourselves to creating a new vision, commit to that vision, declare it out loud, and take action from a foundation of believing in ourselves. So let's use the rest of the chapter to build the skill of envisioning together.

Envisioning: Present Versus Future

It's possible to be fully present and in the moment while also creating a vision—actually, it is required. Planning for and envisioning the future versus worrying about the future are two very different things. You need to take action in the present moment to plan for the desired future outcome. Seeing your vision for the future and taking steps in the present to create it is how a true visionary operates. Worrying, however, is being lost in thoughts about what may or may not happen. You're stuck living in the future, rather than the present moment. Most importantly, worrying is a waste of time! It leaves you immobilized and solves nothing. If you are worrying, you are not creating change or impacting the future. You can only ignite your brilliance and tap into your native genius from the NOW!

Often when I have an idea or a vision, like getting booked to speak and deliver workshops for women leaders in corporate America, I become overwhelmed with the *how-to*. I start thinking, "I don't know how to do this," which can completely paralyze me. Then the worry sets in—how will I pay my bills, am I even capable of this mission, am I good enough…blah, blah, blah, blah. In other words, worry removes me from the present so I cannot tap into my greatest wisdom and take action, and instead it leads me to immobilization and an inability to create my vision.

Taking some sort of action and step forward, even if it is a tiny turtle step towards your dream, is being present and envisioning. Declare it. Even just saying, "I don't know what it is exactly, but I will figure it out as I go," will open up unlimited possibilities. Don't procrastinate by believing you need all the answers first. And don't let your brain fight you. No matter how small a step, it is still one step closer to creating your vision. That momentum leads to the answers you need.

Find the part of you that is waiting to emerge, waiting to be brilliant and shine. Let it out by tuning into what your heart is telling you, and start taking steps to bring it to reality. Everyone has a unique gift they are meant to share with the world and the world needs you to share it. This is the grace within each of us, waiting for permission to emerge.

Grace is often perceived as flow and ease, a soft and sweet quality. But that is only what emanates from grace. Grace is actually pure strength and power—it only appears effortless because it comes from the truth of who you are, your essence, the core of your being. Grace is demonstrated when we let go and open the doors of our heart to reach out into the world and share our unique gift. From the inside out, your foundation is always your core. Think of Pilates. Joseph Pilates developed this series of exercises, based on several foundational yoga principles, to specifically strengthen the core strength of his ballet dancers. He knew the stronger the core, the more graceful the dancer. There could be nothing more graceful than a ballerina, and that grace results from her core strength illuminating outward. The same principle holds true for you as a spiritual being. Living from your center—your core being, or the truth of who you are—positions you to live from your greatest place of strength and grace. Grace *is* pure strength, though it appears effortless and full of ease.

Creating Vision from Your Heart

Step 1: Tune In

People can think and think forever about awakening their passion and discovering their purpose. "Thinking" is the key word here; there is no way to think your way into passion and purpose. Your heart's language speaks to you through feelings, music, art, symbols, and signposts. This information doesn't come from your thinking brain; it is stored in your emotional brain—your heart. So, tuning into your heart requires embodiment, meditation, nature, and play—or any activity that gets you out of your head and tuned into your body and allows you to experience stillness, a reprieve from the chattering mind. For me, my very first yoga class (at age 36) was the first time I clearly remember getting out of my thinking mind and becoming fully present in my body. It was bliss. I distinctly remember saying to myself, "Oh, this is that mind-body-spirit thing!" A pervading sense of peace and stillness came over me—I could hear my heart was speaking to me.

Step 2: Aha Moment

Once you begin tuning into your heart, I promise there will be some aha moments. There will even be some things that might really surprise you, otherwise you wouldn't have locked it way in your body, away from the conscious mind. Maybe your heart will tell you to spend your paycheck on some crazy new animal-print clothing or to take a trip to a disaster relief area. Try not to judge or push it away. You don't have to act on it, just acknowledge it. Let it come up.

Treat your heart with tenderness, the same way you would treat a wounded child. Accept all that comes up. Say kind things to yourself. When you acknowledge your forbidden feelings calmly, you'll find that you actually have more control over your actions. It's when feelings are repressed that they burst out emotionally and behaviorally in dangerous or unhealthy ways.

Living this way takes practice. The more you tune in, the deeper the truths your heart will reveal, the more intense your feelings and emotions get, and the more obvious the direction signs will become in your life. Let anything come up that wants to come up. If pain emerges, let it flow through you and it will be released. You'll find something beneath it, something powerful, the beauty of your true essence—your heart of hearts. Letting the repressed pain come up and flow through was the scariest thing in the world for me. It felt like it would consume me, like I would die and never recover. Mostly I felt as if I wasn't supposed to have these big emotions and that having them made me weak or crazy. The truth is, letting them emerge is a huge release, and a huge feeling of peace follows.

When I went through a month-long residential yoga teacher training in western Massachusetts, there were fourteen women living, breathing, learning, and practicing yoga together six days a week. Almost every day, one of us would have an emotional meltdown, usually with a burst of tears. Often, there was no logical explanation of what it was about. There was an acceptance among all of us that this was totally normal. We were simply unearthing old emotional stuff, and it was coming up to be released.

Step 3: Break Out of Jail

With a regular practice of tuning in to your heart and letting your feelings emerge and flow, you will begin to realize that your heart is your compass and tells you what direction to follow. The next steps will be calling to you, as long as you stay present.

When desire really comes from your heart, deciding to act on it will bring strong sensations. For me, it was an extraordinary feeling of inspiration. I became full of energy and life. Huge emotion swells up within me whenever I state my purpose out loud—it is deep and pure—it is directly from my heart. You will also begin to experience extraordinary clarity, the sense that something inside you has clicked into place. The Jailer (your ego) will try and tell you it is ridiculous, stupid, crazy, and impossible, and that is when you know not to listen. The Jailer is not your heart speaking to you. Your ego always speaks loudest and first. Don't listen. Laugh and run like hell. There is a fine line between fear and excitement, and that line is crossed by breathing through the fear and jumping over into excitement. Dogs are very good at this; they live completely in the moment. If you can't play with it or eat it, pee on it and move on.

Step 4: Jump

Acting on your heart's directions means abandoning all those careful strategies to avoid rejection. Stop following the conventional paths and instead, jump off a cliff with faith and trust, knowing you will grow wings or find a soft place to land. Either way, you will be graceful and open your imagination and then boundless possibilities will emerge.

Taking the enormous risk of freeing and following my heart is the greatest thing I have ever experienced. As a thirteenth century Zen master said, "The place is here. The way leads everywhere." Once you are present in your own *heart*, you'll find your life going places your *mind* never even dreamed possible.

Step 5: Share It

Tell your story. Letting your light shine is how you keep your heart free. You do it by saying your goal out loud, taking action, writing in a journal, and making one small turtle step to activate your vision every day. I developed my vision by creating a feng shui dream board at a party with friends. Not only did it give me something visual to hang on my wall and stay focused on, I ended up declaring out loud to others at the party that I wanted to be a speaker, author, and coach. Even I couldn't believe I was saying it at the time—yet here I am! Telling your story demolishes the barriers between your heart and the outside world. This means that your heart will be exposed and, although it may hurt at times, you will heal. The heart is not imprisoned by being broken, but by being stifled. People thought I was crazy when I told them I was leaving my nice six-figure income with lots of benefits to take a leap of faith into a new career. It is scary at times, but I love who I am now, love how I feel, and have such a sense of freedom because I am living with purpose and passion.

Not knowing your vision is different than not having a vision. In other words, you need to consult your native genius or your heart's desire to become a visionary in your own life. Life's difficulties are always a call to consciousness— grace-inspired events that challenge us to reach beyond our thinking mind. Let's begin.

Exercise: Create Your Inner Vision

Read through and review each step before beginning. I highly recommend you do this with a partner, someone to walk you through the steps verbally. This will allow you to stay fully focused on creating your inner vision without having to read. Find a friend or colleague and do the exercise together, taking turns.

- Sit comfortably, feet firmly planted on the ground, back straight, palms up on your legs, and close your eyes.
- Start bringing your attention to your breath—notice the inhale and exhale.
- With each inhale, imagine breathing in light, joy, love, and peace.
- On each exhale, imagine all doubt or fear flowing out of you and into the core of the earth to be purified.
- Repeat breathing for twelve cycles—twelve inhales and twelve exhales.
- Now, project yourself out five or ten years and begin imagining your life exactly how you want it to be, like you have already achieved your vision and are living it.
- Notice every detail of your life. Don't rush; take as much time as you want; you want to notice as many specifics and details as possible. Allow yourself to dream and let anything come in. Don't question or discern, just let your life unfold; let it flow without judgment. This is a great time to write the details in a journal afterward:
  a. You wake up. What do you see around you, who do you see, how do you feel, what is the view out your window? What does the room look like; how is it decorated?
  b. How do you approach the day? What is your routine? Be specific; what are you doing throughout the morning, what rooms do you go into, what do you eat or drink, do you exercise? See every specific thing as you move, especially your mood and what you are focusing on. Who is around you or with you?
  c. Notice your closet, clothes, and shoes. What are the fabrics and colors, are they seasonal, are they different than your current closet?
  d. Move throughout your day. What are you doing with your time? Notice how you feel energetically, how you look, who you are

interacting with, where you are going, what you are doing, what you are working on, how you are earning a living?

e. Move to the evening and notice every detail from dinnertime until bedtime. Capture how you feel. Gather the essence of what you experience with your inner vision and the physical details.

Exercise: Bring Your Vision into Reality

This exercise should take ten to fifteen minutes. Set some quiet time aside to be alone and complete this next exercise. Don't just read through the steps; actively participate and do them. If you need help, do it with a friend. I'm serious—if you are reading the exercise, but don't have the time to do it right now, schedule twenty minutes in your calendar to come back and do it! This is the beginning of igniting your native genius. It is how you start truly tuning into your heart's desires. This vision exercise can be applied to any aspect of your life and anything you want to create.

1. Today, when you think about creating your vision, what comes to mind? Is it fear or uncertainty? Give it a symbol, something metaphoric in regards to what you feel and see. For example, "I felt like I was in a dark closet and there was no light to lead me to the door; I didn't know how to take action to begin creating my vision."

2. Imagine it is now eighteen months out. Where are you, what are you doing, who is around you, and how are you feeling? Give it another visual symbol that describes how you are feeling and what you are seeing. IMPORTANT NOTE: The only difference between Step 1 and Step 2 is taking some action towards your vision and letting go of limiting thinking. Let go of any "can't, not possible, I don't know how." There is no right or wrong here, and certainly no specific way you are required to do anything. Drop the judgment and allow it to be whatever it wants to be; you may be really surprised at what comes up for you. Just allow infinite

possibilities to open the door and show you the way. Show faith that anything is possible by taking action, no matter how small. Declare your vision out loud to yourself and others. For example, "I saw the light coming in from under the door and now knew which direction to go."

3. You are now a few years out from where you started. You are 80 percent to full realization of the vision you created. Notice what is going on around you, what you are doing, how you are feeling, and who is with you. Most importantly, what is the essence of how you feel? For example, "I was actively climbing a ladder, feeling excited, inspired, and successful. There were lots of women around me and I was speaking and facilitating workshops regularly; I was building programs."

4. You have now fully created your vision; you are living it. What does it look like? What are you doing and feeling? Turn around and look back through the timeline of the previous three steps. What do you notice, what do you see, and how does it feel when you look back to see what got you to where you are today? What stands out? What messages are in those steps that you need to tell yourself NOW? For example, "I am now teaching other women to do what I did. I realized learning and pushing past the fear was necessary so I could teach other women the *how-to*."

5. Write down everything you can remember about your journey. Be as specific as possible.

As you learn to live by heart, every choice you make will become another way of telling your story, calling your tribe, and liberating not only your heart but the hearts of others. This is the very definition of love, the process that makes all-too-human people and societies capable of true humanity. It will chart you a life's journey as unique and authentic as your fingerprint; send you out, full of hope and breathtaking exhilaration, onto paths you never thought you could travel. It is the way you were meant to exist. If you stop to listen, you'll realize that your heart has been telling you so all along.

—**Martha Beck**

Chapter 2

Why We Don't Play BIG

Our deepest fear is not that we are inadequate. Our deepest fear is that we are powerful beyond measure. It is our light, not our darkness, that most frightens us. We ask ourselves, who am I to be brilliant, gorgeous, talented, fabulous? Actually, who are you not to be? You are a child of God. Your playing small doesn't serve the world. There's nothing enlightened about shrinking so that other people won't feel insecure around you. We are all meant to shine, as children do. We were born to make manifest the glory of God that is within us. It's not just in some of us; it's in everyone. And as we let our own light shine, we unconsciously give other people permission to do the same. As we're liberated from our own fear, our presence automatically liberates others.

—Marianne Williamson

Playing Small

W here do you play small? It can happen in any area of your life where you hold back and don't allow inspiration to emerge and marry with taking action. We settle for the comfort zone because it is easier and we can minimize risk. There is, however, no way to expand your life without discomfort and taking risks. Your life unfolds in direct proportion to your level of courage. I say, if you are not expanding, then you are just taking up space and not doing your part to make the world a better place. Not having enough FUN in life is also a big constrictor of creative flow and limitless possibilities. Hard work and drudgery are not the way to creative success and new opportunities. More fun and play open up the world to you.

We do this naturally as children. Notice how children always believe that they can be or do anything. At some point as we move into adulthood our imagination and openness to unlimited possibilities shuts down; passion and pure play seem to become rarities. Ask your girlfriends from high school or college why you don't still explore and belly laugh. Losing that is not part of growing up, yet we somehow make it unimportant as we focus on being responsible and life takes on routine and responsibility.

Why are we so willing to accept "good enough" instead of going for "great?" One reason is that many of us are programmed from a very early age to simply get by, to get a good job, work hard, start a family, and then live for overindulgent weekends as a way to escape the "no-fun" grind and struggle of Monday through Friday. But human beings aren't meant to just survive the "hamster wheel of life," to just make it through the day and then get up the next day to do it all over again. We are meant to thrive! We are meant to live in a way that allows Monday through Sunday to be all about living fully and having fun.

Most of us weren't taught to go after our dreams, and we certainly weren't taught to dream BIG! Instead, we were taught to follow suit on what a good life was supposed to mean, and we were not encouraged to think big and play often. Having a dream and taking action on it is how we thrive and enjoy life.

In our culture, the words *dream* and *fantasy* have almost become synonymous. Yet there is a big difference. A *dream* is your soul or spirit calling you to take action to create more joy and abundance for yourself and bring healing to the world. You have control over making your dreams come true. A *fantasy* is a hope or a wish that may or may not happen, but you have NO control over making it happen. For example, winning the lottery is a fantasy.

The truth is, it's usually our fears that are the fantasy. Yet we say we're just being "realistic." People used to be afraid they would fall off the edge of the earth, so they stayed small by not venturing out. Imagine our lives today if no one had been willing to discover what lay beyond the edge of the known world! Ask yourself what you are missing out on because you play small and don't open to new possibilities? Could some of your fears be fantasies? What has being "realistic" cost you in your life regarding experience and joy?

When we play it small and play it safe, we hold ourselves back and can't shine our light. I believe there are four common traps that women fall into, which hold them back from playing big: 1) perfectionism, 2) being other focused, 3) proving our competence, and 4) not using our voice.

Perfectionism

Women have become so attached to being perfect and looking perfect that we miss the vast possibilities in our life. Being perfect or appearing perfect is about controlling the perception of others. It is an unattainable attempt to look and do everything right. It has nothing to do with striving for excellence and *healthy* self-focused achievement; it's about the need to gain approval from others. No one can find joy, freedom, or success through perfectionism. In fact, there is no way to discover our gifts, passion, and purpose while pursuing perfection. The road of perfectionism is a big-ass detour from finding our truth. Even over-planning kills creativity and then the magic is lost; the unlimited possibilities are no longer available for us to see. Perfectionism actually inhibits success, as it is not motivation to achieve and grow. It keeps us small and constricted, as if we can only play within the confines of a box. It is an addiction, a never-ending attempt to avoid blame, judgment, and shame, and to get praise.

Be willing to take risks, fail, and put yourself out there. Let go of the fear of not looking good. This is the way to determine what is truly possible so you can grow. The manifestation of success can happen when you let yourself out of the box of perfection. You have to be willing to go all out (and maybe even suck at it). It's how we learn, grow, and discover our greatness—then we play big. Creativity and infinite possibilities flow to you when you play and explore, not when you strive for perfection. Give yourself permission to not be perfect, to not have all the answers up front, but still take a step out. This is one of the greatest gifts you could offer yourself and it will most likely lead to an outcome even greater than what you originally thought possible. This is the path of growth and improvement. It is the path of the free.

I know it is not easy. It takes courage and the willingness to look bad or do things that may appear unsuccessful. Let go of what others think, and let yourself play and practice. This became really clear to me recently in a coaching course I took. We often had training sessions where we coached the coach, meaning one trainee was coaching another trainee as if they were a client. Usually we were practicing a specific coaching tool. At first, it was really intimidating for me to coach someone in front of my peers, knowing I would be critiqued. I was scared of not doing it perfect, not looking like I was good at it. Then one of the master coaches said to me, "Just do it and be willing to suck. That is how you learn and that is how you will become a great coach. You can't learn by attempting to look perfect." And it worked! It was exactly what I needed to hear to put myself in the arena without trying to be perfect.

Let go of the never-enough syndrome, the need for approval, and the desire to set unrealistic expectations for yourself. Really. Just let it go so you may open the doors to all kinds of new possibilities. There is no such thing as perfection anyway; it is a trap that keeps you from experiencing your true greatness. Instead, focus on all the things you do well and the times you get it right. Find approval and acknowledgement for yourself every day. What we put our attention on grows. It's a simple equation; you want to grow more of what you already do well. Put your focus on what you want and what you have done well. As a woman, I've noticed how hard it is to recognize our wins and celebrate them. I cannot emphasize enough how important it is to acknowledge your accomplishments. Instead, we focus on what we haven't done yet or don't do well. We focus on what we lack, instead of what makes us great. Stop that now! Actively give yourself credit where credit is due. Pat yourself on the back and recognize your accomplishments. It is so easy to focus on what we haven't done or what needs to be done, and move forward without first acknowledging our achievements. Don't miss this step—celebrate your victories before you focus on where you still need improvement.

Learn to actively acknowledge your successes in life. Schedule regular calls with colleagues, peers, or friends for support in business and life. Find a friend that is willing to set the tone at the beginning of your calls by sharing something you can celebrate, any kind of success or accomplishment from the prior week, small or large. You'll find this starts putting the focus on what's great in your life and help you to keep the momentum going. Most importantly, you will be actively acknowledging and giving yourself credit for what you get right.

Proving Competence

Closely related to perfectionism is the need to prove our competence, or to get permission from someone else before we act. As women in the business world, we have allowed ourselves to become guided by the linear, masculine way of thinking, and have focused most of our energy trying to prove ourselves competent instead of selling our vision. In other words, we don't give ourselves permission to PLAY BIG! Sheryl Sandberg did a great job with her book *Lean In* (Knopf, 2013), sharing how women focus on proving themselves competent or having 100 percent of the experience boxes checked before they put themselves out there. Sheryl's term "leaning in" describes how women can break through a self-imposed glass ceiling when it comes to parity with men in the workplace. In other words, women focus on what they lack, not what they can bring. Men, on the other hand, will put themselves out there and go for it even when they only possess 60 percent of the experience needed. They will lead with what they can add to a project or position without focusing on what they lack. They often won't even consider where they fall short. They will confidently take risks and trust they will figure out what they need to know as they go. This hit me like a ton of bricks. I realized how true it was, as I had observed it over and over again through my own friends and colleagues. I also realized that I had been "leaning in" for years but instead had always called it "leaning forward."

Leaning forward was a survival mechanism I developed as a child due to my own inferiority complex and feelings of inadequacy. At age eight, when my father had died, and until my early teen years, I experienced a lot of suffering believing there was something wrong with me. As my physical beauty began to blossom as a teenager and I started drawing some positive attention to myself, I latched on to what I saw as successful and strong families and began mimicking their behavior. I saw them as showing up in the world with polish, class, and a regal strength. Whenever I was in a situation where I felt inferior, I would immediately adopt a confident and head-held-high persona. This is a very real example of how the "act as if" strategy really works. One day the confidence turns out to be real, and this is exactly how it became my truth in my career. I had learned to plow forward with confidence, focusing on what I wanted to be, not who I wasn't.

I was a physical education major in college. Yep, I have a PE degree! It was what I loved, and I thought, at the time, I would become a high school swim coach. I ended up working in the fitness industry for a while, primarily in sales. From there, I transferred my sales skills to technology sales. When I landed my first professional job at Tech Data Corporation, the company was about a $1 billion-per-year IT distributor. They were the middleman, selling and distributing products for manufacturers like HP and Microsoft to IT solution providers that install networks and computers for companies.

Needless to say, back in 1988, this was a big stretch for me. I didn't have a technical or business background, but when I interviewed, I knew I really wanted the job and told myself, "I've got this, it's mine." I never once thought I didn't have the skills set or experience. I knew I could sell and I was purely focused on the fact that I was excited about getting the job and knew I had the passion to make it work. I was confident I could figure it out as I went—and I did. Then came an even bigger jump. I went to work for InFocus, a projector manufacturer, managing the Tech Data relationship.

The step up that came next was even bigger still. I was golfing with a few friends from the industry and heard that a Cisco account manager job was open. Cisco is an enterprise networking manufacturer. My eyes got big, and I said, "Oh that is so mine!" This was a giant step for any low-experience manufacturer's rep. I ended up getting the job, which led to another huge increase in pay and position within four years of being back in the workforce after taking five years off to be home with my kids. Even taking myself out of the career track and not having a business and technical education couldn't hold me back, because I never considered those things to be limiting. I focused on what I could bring and also realized that what I didn't have, I could figure out or learn as I moved upward.

This is a behavior and attitude any one can learn. *Act as if* can be applied to any part of life when learning something new. It is not being a fraud; it is aligning yourself with what you want to achieve while you master the skills set. It is adopting the feeling "as if" you have already achieved the desired goal or outcome. I learned this as a survival mechanism to hold my ground in the world. I think most men learn it because they are conditioned and taught to take risk, act strong, and compete—and then they just begin to do it naturally.

The second piece to propelling yourself through the self-created glass ceiling is to focus on what positives you already possess and where you can bring value, de-emphasizing or not bringing attention to what you perceive as lacking experience, answers, and credentials. It is about moving forward and taking action in the face of fear when passion or excitement is present.

Pursue competence by leaning forward into opportunities. Competence doesn't happen by having all your ducks in a row or all the boxes checked. Competence comes from excitement, desire, confidence, and willingness to learn as you go. It's simple and all about focusing on what you can bring, not what you haven't done yet.

Being Others Focused

This is a huge problem for most women, as it limits our ability to take action for ourselves, so our life can reflect our desires and dreams. It stems from the misbelief that "me first" is selfish. We are brought up and conditioned as women to be caretakers of everyone else, but not of ourselves. We have become attached to getting validation through helping, supporting, aiding, and holding others up so they can shine while sacrificing ourselves in the process. "Me first" is actually the most loving thing you could do for yourself and those in your life. When you take care of you, it not only allows you to have more energy to be there for others, it offers others the role modeling to take responsibility for themselves. When we focus on taking care of others first, it is like trying to constantly fill a cup with holes in it. We have to fill our own holes first so there is plenty of water to share with others. Taking care of you first is the most important thing you can do for you and all those you love. It is critical to your empowerment and happiness. As they say in pre-flight instructions, "Put your own oxygen mask on first, before attempting to help others." Amen, sister!

The other piece of being other focused is that we give our power away by concerning ourselves with what others think about us and whether they like and approve of us. I see women adopting the role of peacemaker and putting approval and being liked in front of being heard or speaking their truth. They are sacrificing their voice and truth in order to make others okay with who they are. Do you sacrifice your own happiness by trying to make others think you are happy? I see this every day. It is a prison of the mind, a prison with self-imposed bars that don't even exist. The greatest freedom is letting go of caring about what other people think of you. Start focusing on what you think of you. Are you living in a way that you can love and approve of yourself? If you love who you are and align with your truth, then whether someone likes you or doesn't won't matter either way, because you are okay with you. When you are your ideas, and behavior, then you don't need anyone else to love them. Focusing on what others think about you cannot ever bring you peace or joy, and there is no way to be aligned with your inner wisdom or find your passion and purpose. When we are in love with our own choices and behavior, we don't care or need other people to love those choices and behaviors.

Finding Your Voice

Not using your voice to speak your truth or stand in your power is one of the greatest ways we hold ourselves back. As Western women, we have the ability to use our voice freely, unlike many women in other parts of the world. We are already empowered, but we need to claim that voice not only for ourselves, but to help empower every woman on the planet.

I have noticed younger generations of women, especially teens and women in their 20s, actively keeping each other oppressed through sexual exploitation and pretending to act stupid. They are disempowering themselves. During my corporate experience, I saw women not bond together in support of raising each other up, but view each other as competition, as if there was a limited amount of success to go around. Meaning, if you get a piece of the pie, there is less pie for me.

This focus on lack comes from a purely physical perspective, as opposed to opening ourselves to the possibilities we all possess from a spiritual perspective. We are not just human beings, but spiritual beings. When we honor one another and care about the greater good and creating impact, anything can unfold for us. I don't believe in lack; for me, "lack" is simply another term for limited possibilities. I don't buy into what the news says or what the economy says and allow their perceived "lack" to become my reality of possibilities. If you believe the economy is tough and you will have difficulty finding a job or getting a promotion, guess what, you'll get to be right! If you believe that women in the world are your competition, they will be, as that is what you will set up and create. Viewing each other as competition fosters an atmosphere of using our voice to criticize, compare, and gossip about one another. This is one of the most disempowering things we do to each other every day.

So men are not the ones keeping us down; we often do it to ourselves. We inherently oppress each other as women when we view each other as competition, especially in the corporate world, but also socially. We are failing to acknowledge and honor the divine feminine power that resides in each of us. I believe many women flee the corporate world to become entrepreneurs to become free to express themselves, and to flee this competition. I find nothing more unnerving than hearing a man comment, "I love a good cat fight." Men say women can be so vicious to one another, and it's true. Men have one up on us here: they speak out, say what they need to say, and it's over.

We must start using our voices to promote ourselves and each other. The perspective that we are competing with each other has to shift to a perspective that we gain strength and power by supporting each other. We are all responsible for creating this tidal wave of change in the world by invoking the feminine power, but this can't happen if women view each other as competition. I highly encourage you to STOP criticizing, comparing, and gossiping about other women—or anyone, for that matter. When you catch yourself doing it or getting caught up in it with others, shut it down and help bring attention to this behavior to the other women involved. Girls behaving badly are not sexy, powerful, or attractive. Nothing good can come from it. I have certainly participated in this behavior, and I now do my best never to start it or get sucked into it. I have also been a recipient of this behavior, and it is painful. Participating can only offer a very temporary and artificial good feeling, based on the illusion that you have elevated yourself above others.

This behavior is no different than bullying. How do you think kids learn it? Bullying is an attempt to feel better about yourself by putting others down and taking the attention off of you. It doesn't make you better, and there is nothing productive that comes from it. It is not kind, loving, nor supportive. It is absolutely not aligned with your light and the truth of who you are.

Great leaders always want to lift others up into the light where they reside. They want to support others and guide others with integrity to help them develop their potential and reach their goals. To drive change, we need to create a bond of sisterhood, and the best place to start is within. So be a leader here. Don't participate, and have the courage to bring it to the attention of others when you witness this behavior. Use your voice for greatness, for strength, and for the positive promotion of yourself and each other. Speak up about what you know is right and loving, and use your powerful words for the greater good.

And make sure to speak up in both your business and personal life! In the business arena, I have heard women comment that they held back sharing an opinion or view in a meeting because they were fearful of ridicule or non-acceptance. To help them get "out of the box," many people just need to hear a voice sharing a view outside the norm. When we hold back voicing a feeling, a thought, an opinion, or an intuition that could help shape something to be great, we not only do a disservice to ourselves, but to the world.

I learned for myself that in male-dominated meetings, when something came up that I wanted to share and provoked an adrenaline rush, due to the fear of not being mainstream or agreeing with the conversation, I knew I absolutely had to share it. It was important for me to push past the fear and speak up. I encourage you to tune into the place that is calling you to speak up when you feel it emerging from a deeper place than just your intellect or the conventional norms.

I cannot emphasize enough how vital this behavior is for the world. Holding back your voice is never serving anyone; it is simply creating more deficiencies. Be willing to be different; take the chance that your opinion or idea might not be accepted. It's okay! The more you speak up and put things out there, the more you give permission to others to do the same and the more success we will have in changing the language of the business meeting. If you find yourself holding back out of fear of what people will think, *that* is your compass telling you, "SAY IT!"

I often wonder how much creativity and innovation gets stifled in the world for exactly this reason. We don't unleash progress because of fear of making a mistake, not sounding smart, or not being approved of by others. This imprisonment of our voice is making us robots and jailkeepers of each other. Using your voice in the face of fear when you have something positive or different to say is one of the greatest forms of freedom and empowerment.

As a woman that has done well speaking up in the business world, I struggled immensely with speaking up for myself in romantic relationships. It took me many years of pain and suffering, and then therapy, personal, and spiritual development, before I learned to stand in my power and use my voice with a partner. I was so afraid of not being loved and of being abandoned, that I abandoned myself emotionally in an attempt to keep the love I found (which usually wasn't love at all). It was a liberating experience for me to find my truth and voice it.

I still see many girlfriends struggle with this today, and I saw it as the norm in my mother's generation. Friends whose lives revolve around their husband, put their needs second to accommodate their spouse and ensure he is loved and taken care of first. These are women that don't speak up for themselves, nor do they express their needs or what works for them. They bury their voice to keep peace, to be loved, at the expense of their own health and well-being. Withholding your voice when there is a need to express yourself and live the truth of who you are will eventually show up in your health. If you look at anyone you know that has health issues around the throat, like thyroid problems or tumors, and autoimmune diseases, I am willing to bet they don't speak up for themselves or speak their truth. Their repressed voice needs to be heard in order to heal. Often it is unexpressed anger turned inward.

The voice is one of our most powerful strengths. Use it wisely, with meaning and purpose, to express the depth of who you are and to speak for those that cannot speak for themselves. Use your voice as a creative expression for the greater good, to support other women and mankind as a whole. Let your voice be the inspiration you use for yourself and to motivate others.

Part Two

WAKE UP YOUR
NATIVE GENIUS AND EMERGE

We are given choices every day. There can be wisdom in every choice we make in our life; even when we make a choice that creates an unwanted consequence, there is wisdom to be gained. Choices are like a set of doors in front of us—we pick one and the others close, but then a new set of doors opens. It is always a choice: where we go, what we do, how we show up for ourselves, and how we react to situations or others.

What is in your soul's purpose in life? What is your life art? How can you help leave the world a better place? Only you can discover this for yourself. These are the questions that determine your depth of character and the choices you make, your authentic expression. It's everyone's responsibility to contribute, to help relieve suffering and to teach joy. Transformation begins with learning to live from your core strength. The second step is to become fully embodied or present. There is no way to make this shift to the mind-body-spirit connection without becoming a whole being. This is not a "thinking" shift; you can't *think* your way into wisdom and purpose.

Chapter 3

Here's To Letting Go

"When you follow your bliss…doors will open where you would not have thought there would be doors, and where there wouldn't be a door for anyone else."

—Joseph Campbell

hat is the purpose of life? We are taught to believe it's about upward social mobility, establishing a career, accumulating wealth, and competing and winning. It's all we know.

Real purpose is actually something quite different. Real purpose means living authentically and discovering who you are, not changing yourself or even "becoming" yourself, but "uncovering" yourself. Your gift or purpose in the world is as unique to you as your DNA and fingerprint. It is not one specific task or thing to create; it is how you are meant to show up in the world each and every day. Your purpose is always evolving and is always calling you. Life itself has no meaning; you bring meaning by discovering the vital you and living it outwardly to fulfill your purpose. Purpose is spirit seeking expression, your unique destiny. As you live out your destiny, you'll find you take each moment more *and* less seriously because you understand that everything passes, both the joyful moments and the difficult ones.

So your real purpose is not about attaining anything. It's about letting go of your external definitions of purpose so your beauty can shine through.

Let Go of Your Job

Let's start with making the transition from viewing your work as a job to viewing it as a calling. A job is doing a set of tasks for pay. A calling is an organic field of energy that emerges from the deepest aspects of who you are. It is passionate and compulsive. This doesn't mean you have to change careers or start your own business, though it could mean that. Whatever work you do right now can be your transition point by reframing how you view it and how you show up every day to do your work. It's not about the achieving, but about coming into being. Instead of focusing purely on making money, focus instead on being of value and creating impact. Money is a result that will manifest naturally—it should not be the focus or goal.

People often mistakenly believe that finding their calling means you have to find some really big thing to create, therefore they never get around to finding it or even starting. In actuality, a calling is anything that provokes passion and comes from the depth of your soul. It has deep meaning to you, you feel more expansive and lighter when you do it, and most importantly, you are in some way making the world a better place. Contributing to the greater good can be as simple as doing one small act of kindness daily, giving a small gift of thoughtfulness to people in your life, or making a point to be generous with your time with someone that could greatly benefit.

I searched for my calling (or dharma) for several years, as if it was going to be some big discovery, project, or career change that would finally feed my soul. But finding your calling doesn't have to be big—you just have to play big. You can turn your current job into a calling today, by changing how you show up and knowing that you are good enough just because you exist on this planet. Be a role model to others instead of shrinking yourself and acting as if you're sorry for being there—that is playing small. The easiest way to transition your work from a job to a calling is by making your work your ministry. This has nothing to do with religion. It is purely about being the best you that you can be at any given moment and sharing yourself with your whole heart. It is everyone's responsibility to pursue their passion, to find their calling and be more loving, kind, and compassionate. Serving the world in any way that invokes passion is your calling. It is your *life art* and it is how you truly play big.

Let Go of Conformity

We are taught and raised to live from the outside in, instead of from the inside out. This means we seek guidance from others and live for approval. We adopt behaviors and make choices based on what others do and think. We live for approval from parents, society, and our community. Sometimes what we do is done out of pure unconscious habit, based on what our role models did, without ever questioning if it even works for us or makes us happy. We can often invest huge amounts of energy into an activity or certain way of behaving simply because that is how it has always been done.

Here is a simple yet pointed story of how this happens to each of us in everyday life. There once was a woman who had a particular ritual for cooking her holiday ham. Before placing the ham in a roasting pan to bake, she always cut off the end. After many years of observing the ritual, one day her husband finally asked why she always removed the end of the ham before baking. Her reply was simply, "I don't know; that's how I saw my mother do it when I was a child." The woman then became curious as to why her mother performed this task, and asked her. The reply from her mother was simple: "Because at the time, I didn't own a pan big enough to accommodate the large ham."

How many things in your life are purely done on autopilot, based on what you learned or observed without questioning whether or not it makes sense or if it suits you?

I had a girlfriend I knew from a playgroup when our kids were young, and at the time, I really didn't know anything about the Catholic religion that she practiced. The extent of my knowledge was noticing as a child that the Catholic families were always the ones with most kids on the block. Then came my friend Denise. She was adamant about never missing Saturday evening mass, no matter what. I thought this was such an astonishing commitment and assumed it must be such an amazing experience every Saturday evening. I asked her one day why it was so important for her to attend mass every Saturday. Was it that inspirational? Did she just love her priest? Her response was: "No, I don't even like going. It is boring and the current priest is actually kind of a jerk. " Of course I asked her, "Well, why the hell do you go every Saturday?" Denise replied, "It is just what I have always done." I know that to anyone raised Catholic, this might seem like an obvious or typical answer, but I was flabbergasted. I am not picking on religion here, only using it as an example of what stood out to me when I first began to investigate conformity for myself and why I did some of the things I did.

Here's another example: While pregnant with my son, I watched a film in childbirth class about how circumcision was performed. I was mortified! It overwhelmed me to even consider placing my newly born infant on a board, strapping him down, and then mutilating the most sensual, sexual part of his body. With no anesthesia to boot. It seemed like medieval torture, but it was 1993. I also felt it was not my right to make this decision for him, and I didn't understand the arrogance of changing the way a human being comes into the world naturally. This sent me off on a research project, to find some logical reason as to why I should conform.

I found the United States is pretty much the only country in the world that circumcises for non-religious reasons. It was originally started as a standard practice during the Victorian era to avoid infection (when people didn't bathe regularly) and because it was believed it would keep boys from masturbating during a time that sex was taboo. Soap and water are no longer an issue in our country, and I am pretty sure nothing has changed with boys and their desire to masturbate. Circumcision was standard practice prior to the 1990s and didn't even require parental consent. Yet, it was not medically necessary. People just went along with it, like a herd of cattle, because it was what had always been done, what they were told to do. I couldn't go along with the herd; it felt wrong to me. It didn't require much explanation to my son and he was grateful we didn't do it. I was on the leading edge of changing this norm, as my son was in the 10 percent of US boys in the 1990s that weren't circumcised. The rebellion against this particular conformity is still on the rise today.

The above example is in no way meant to be a judgment on anyone's choice. There is no right or wrong in the choice itself, it is a personal choice, but *choice* is the optimal word here. What is important is that we learn to make a conscious choice, as opposed to doing what everyone else does without questioning if it is right or wrong for us. We can all do things just because it is what we were taught, or it was the example shown to us, or we have never investigated further to know something else existed or was possible. But if you are only following the herd, then you are asleep at the wheel of your life or a sheep in the herd. Why do human beings so readily and easily accept certain things and behave in certain ways without question? We behave from the *outside in*, not from love and joy, the place that is inherent in all of us—the *inside out*. It is common for us to deny who we are to live someone else's script in life. This is conformity over truth. Living from conditioning versus being awake.

We even look to others for guidance with something as personal as our life purpose. No one can truly know our purpose but our own spirit, our own inner guru, God, our higher self, or whatever term resonates with you. We are taught to look for a career before we look for a calling. It is the societal checklist: pick a school, develop a career path, find a partner, buy a house, and have kids. The American dream is all about conformity and teaches that happiness is a result of outside achievements, rather than internal ones. Our desires and lives are driven by marketing and advertising, especially in the

United States. It's a constant bombardment of messages telling us that we need to seek fulfillment and find rewards outside of ourselves, like wealth, status, sex, fame, power, winning, and approval.

There is an Asian folklore demon called the hungry ghost. It has an endless and ravenous stomach with a tiny pinhole mouth. Because the hungry ghosts can never eat enough to satisfy, they are on an endless journey of devouring. They are grabby and needy. Somebody once asked the Vietnamese Zen Buddhist monk Thich Nhat Hanh, "What does the realm of the hungry ghost look like?" He replied with one word: "America."

We are meant to live a life full of abundance, but when we live looking from the outside in instead of the inside out, there will be no deep fulfillment or peace. Our freedom is found in discovering the truth in our own heart and spirit, not from a mold that was given to us.

Let Go of Avoiding Discomfort

As a life coach, I quickly realized that the one constant, no matter what an individual's life circumstances or desires may be, is there is no way to grow or create transformation without feelings of discomfort. Yet the human default response to feeling discomfort is to avoid it at all costs. It is counter-intuitive to willingly go into feelings of discomfort, yet that is exactly how we move through difficult situations or circumstances in life. Feeling and allowing yourself to experience a place of discomfort is absolutely necessary to learn, grow, and evolve. This ranges from the discomfort in trying a new activity, ending a relationship, grieving the loss of a loved one, or facing and healing childhood wounds or shame. Avoiding uncomfortable feelings and pain in any area of life ultimately keeps us stuck and prevents us from finding our joy. Learning to be brazen in our own lives leads us to our greatness. Finding a comfort in discomfort is how we normalize the experience and make it something we don't have to avoid or fear.

When I launched my career as a speaker, I joined a local women's Toastmasters group. This provided a great place to practice and speak to an audience representative of the larger groups I would reach, and it provided valuable feedback. The core purpose of Toastmasters is to help people become stronger and more confident public speakers and presenters. Giving feedback and constructive criticism is part of the organization and is expected. Yet I see members avoid sharing negative or uncomfortable feedback that would be very helpful for growth. The group as a whole seems to focus mostly on providing encouragement, which is important, but the hard-to-hear feedback is often omitted or left unsaid. I think this is because people don't want to make anyone uncomfortable.

I also hear about people avoiding their discomfort from grief every day. It is now encouraged to take anti-depressants or anti-anxiety medication when someone is grieving. Grief is uncomfortable, but there is no way to get to the other side and gain acceptance if you don't allow yourself to feel and process the journey. Numbing out to grief stunts emotional growth. We have become so accustomed to avoiding discomfort in our society that we now attempt to go numb to the natural stages of life, death of a loved one, and the ending of a relationship.

Normalizing discomfort as a part of our culture would benefit society as a whole. We all want to become better, stronger, and add more value in many aspects of life—work, school, and family. Valuable feedback is necessary to foster growth and transformation. Learning how to provide this feedback to others is just as important. When we don't receive authentic comments, we check out and begin to just go through the motions. This is where process begins superseding human value, connection, and creativity.

It is not going to be comfortable to hear that you need to improve in a certain area, that you need to stop doing something, that you could do a better job if you changed, or even that your life has changed. But we can make it a normal part of life to feel uncomfortable, instead of avoiding it like the plague. It is only an experience; it won't kill you. Feeling uncomfortable is the only way to change, grow, and expand your life. If life's purpose is to evolve, then discomfort needs to be seen as part of the process and should be completely normal during transformation. The reward of facing discomfort is greater performance, strength, and the gift of joy!

Let Go of Limiting Thoughts and Beliefs

⤜⤛⤚⤙⤘⤗

"You must do the thing you think you cannot do."

—**Eleanor Roosevelt**

⤖⤗⤘⤙⤚⤛

I believe all suffering comes from the beliefs and thoughts we carry. We have carried most of them so long that we don't even realize they are part of us; they are so deep in our subconscious that we have accepted them as who we are, as if these beliefs and thoughts are part of our true nature. But a belief is simply something you hold to be true. It is not fact. Beliefs are our personal religions. So why are the majority of people so willing to accept beliefs as fact, without any investigation or exploration as to whether they serve us or inhibit us from experiencing a fuller and more loving, joyous life?

Look in your own home, for instance. Let's say you hang a new picture or you decorate a room. After many months or years, you no longer even notice or pay any particular attention to the room or the things in it—they are just there. We become so accustomed to seeing the room that it becomes unconscious background, and we become almost numb to what's there. The same holds true with beliefs and thoughts we have been holding onto for a very long time. They are now there unnoticed and unquestioned. You are so used to them, you are desensitized to how they are affecting you and your life. There is a comfort in what we know. These stories become our identity. The longer we hold a belief and particular thought pattern, the harder it is to become conscious of them and make a change. It is as if the beliefs and patterns can almost become hardwired in our brain.

This unconscious way of living, not being aware of the beliefs that are driving your thoughts, which then ultimately drive your feelings and behavior, is where most humans live today. We live on the surface of life, numb, going through the motions, occupy ourselves with distractions, and doing whatever possible to keep pain suppressed. In most cases, we don't even know we are avoiding feelings and emotions. This may be part of the reason why addictions are at an all-time high. In general, we have very dissatisfied and mildly depressed people at the highest numbers ever. Below are some self-reflective or introspective questions I learned from my Martha Beck Life Coach Training. They are designed to help you reach your feelings of suffering or areas of dissatisfaction in life. Pain and dissatisfaction are based in beliefs and thoughts. They need to be examined and changed or upgraded in order to allow more freedom and joy to flow into your life. Feeling sadness at times due to life circumstances is normal. However, ongoing feelings of suffering or dissatisfaction are not normal. Pain is inevitable; suffering is optional.

Examples of dissatisfaction:

- running on empty, just existing, feeling unfulfilled, going through the motions
- thinking "is this it?"
- putting on a happy face, but feeling sad inside
- having it all, yet still feeling unhappy
- putting everyone's needs before yours, if you even get to yours at all
- feeling like your life is in shambles, like you're in a constant struggle

Your thoughts, actions, and behaviors create your reality. What you put your attention on grows. Energy follows attention. Setting intention of what you want to create in your life is critical. Backing that intention up with supportive thoughts, actions, and behaviors is necessary to create the desired outcome.

Thoughts. The Henry Ford quote, "Whether you think you can or think you can't—you're right," is the most powerful thing I could say to express the importance of the quality of your thoughts. It's important that you begin to understand the power of your thoughts in regards to how they contribute to what you create. My mother would often say to me, "Thoughts are things." I never understood what she really meant until I was probably age 40. Consider what I said earlier when I explained how I went after my next career move.

My thoughts were affirmative: *I want this, I've got this.* That is truly all I was thinking. I did not think: *I am not qualified, I do not have enough experience.* If I had thought those things, I probably wouldn't have gotten the jobs or even allowed myself to go after them. I believed I could, and I was right. Start tuning into what you are thinking by asking yourself, "Am I telling myself I can, or I can't?"

Actions. Will is what allows you to take action. There is a lot to be said for the Nike slogan, "Just Do It." I apply that to so many areas of my life. *Thinking* about getting my running shoes on and heading out the front door is easy, actually doing it is different. I will procrastinate, come up with excuses, find distractions, and then beat myself up for not doing it. When I am avoiding what I need to do for myself, I can suddenly make cleaning the cat box a priority. It is only sheer *will* that gets me moving. Once I start running, I am all in and then so happy afterwards. I feel great physically and feel good about myself. Sitting down to write every day required the same kind of will—just sitting down was the hardest part. Once I got focused and started typing, I was all in and the words started flowing. What if every time you told yourself, "I should…," you actually did it?

I've also noticed that the longer anyone goes without taking action, the harder it is to get back in the game. I learned through my coaching training to set small goals—goals that feel really easy to accomplish and don't make me squirm when I think about tackling them. I also provide myself with a little reward when I complete the small step or goal; things like getting a latte, walking around the block with my dog, or calling a friend to chat. The key for setting up your goals is to make them small enough that you feel like, "No problem; I can do that!" Make small turtle steps so you don't feel overwhelmed, anxious, or dreadful. Any size step will take you forward and closer to your goal. No action gets you nowhere.

My small, manageable goal was writing 700 words a day, yet often the momentum took over and I would end up writing 1,200 to 1,500 words. Like I said, it's just getting your shoes on and getting out the door (where the *will* comes in) and then the action takes on a life of its own. Make your will to "just do it" a part of your strategy to take action in your life.

It's a matter of just saying to yourself, "Get off your butt and get it done." Push through the resistance, because you will feel so much better about yourself after you do and it will lead you to creating whatever it is you want in life.

Behaviors. Your behaviors need to be congruent with what you want to create or achieve. In other words, does your outward behavior match your inspired vision? As you learn to follow your heart and take action from an inner knowing, your attitude is in alignment. The path then becomes full of ease, once you get over the initial hump of starting. I think that as a rule of thumb, men generally take action very easily and quickly, but their behaviors are not always a reflection of their inner knowing or wisdom. Women, on the other hand, are often in touch with that knowing and wisdom, but don't take action to bring it into fruition. In either case, our behaviors are not congruent with the truth of who we are and living with purpose and passion. For example, if you want to lose weight and get physically fit for your health and wellbeing, your behaviors would be aligned with your goals if you started eating clean and exercising regularly. If you kept eating fried chicken and sugary foods and weren't making a strong attempt to exercise, then your goals and your behavior aren't congruent. There is no right or wrong; just match what you say you want with your behavior. It is the best way to build integrity within yourself and to feel self-love. You learn to trust *you*.

Forced behavior is not in alignment with your heart either. Force is different than using a little *will* to get into action. The easiest way to know when your behavior is in alignment with your heart is if the path is filled with a sense of ease and accomplishment. Behaviors driven by force will lead to a path filled with obstacles that hinder us at nearly every turn. Can you think of a time that you forced something to happen, and it created struggles and obstacles? If this happens, you will know you are going against the grain of your path or inner truth.

Because I am so action oriented, I can get really focused on getting something done, and my behavior becomes completely task-oriented by checking off the boxes. In other words, I resort to pure force without taking time to slow down and check if the behaviors are reflective of my best interests. I can be planning a trip and taking care of all the details like flights and accommodations and I just get it done without really checking in with my deeper wisdom. This has meant a lot of plane tickets I didn't use. Once, I was going to open a yoga studio and was attacking the startup with a fury of speed. When I got to the point of leasing a space, I hit one obstacle after another and every opportunity fell through for the most obscure reason. This finally got me to stop moving, out of pure frustration. Within a few months, many things in my personal life went wacky. My 14-year-old daughter became very troubled, and my fiancé returned home from Iraq with nearly out-of-control PTSD. Had I forced the opening of a yoga studio, I would have been on a path of struggle; it wouldn't have been right for me and my life. Finding your center to drive your behavior is how you align with inspiration.

Other times, we may overthink our decisions, choosing the guidance of the mind over the messages of the heart. Overthinking can lead to paralysis where behavior is stifled and no action is being taken. This creates many missed opportunities and growth. One of my mother's famous sayings was, "Right, wrong, do something." I see women struggle to make decisions and take action in their lives on a regular basis, whether it is buying a car or looking for a better job. Overthinking becomes an endless circle, round and round with no decision to do something. The thinking mind doesn't have the answers of where you need to go; your wisdom or heart knows. Learning to hear the message, trust it, and behave in accordance with the message by taking action is always the right and best choice. Even a not-so-great decision is better than no decision. You can learn from poor decisions; therefore, there are no wrong decisions. Taking out the possibility that there is a *wrong* decision will free you up to take action.

Ask yourself these questions below to discover the beliefs and thoughts behind your feelings and experiences.[7] Write your answers on a separate page and don't hold back!

- What do you do in your life that you dislike or even hate, but you tell yourself you "have to"? Make a list of these.

- Now go through each of your "hate to, but have to" items and ask yourself: Do I *really* have to?
- If the answer is yes, remind yourself that there are honestly very few things in life we have to do. Most often we decide we "have to" do these things because of internalized rules from our personal religions (which are enforced by the all-knowing "everybody"—or it is the "proper" thing to do).
- Ask yourself: "Why do I think I have to do this thing I dislike so much?" Write this next to each "hate to," but "have to" item on your list. If the answers are "because my boss says so," "because it's written in the Bible," or "because I don't want to hurt someone's feelings," then ask yourself, "why would that be so bad?" In other words, why would it be so bad to go against what your boss said or hurt someone's feelings? Asking *why* enough times (usually 3-5) gets you to what is truly driving your behavior or choice.
- If your answers to why it would be so bad are something like "I can't get fired," "that wouldn't be nice," or "that person will be mad at me," then really ask yourself—why would that be a problem?

You are ultimately asking yourself "why" to help uncover your belief system, rather than focusing on the outside world. The point is to keep asking yourself "why?" to take you four or five levels deep to get to the *real* reason why you hate to or have to do something. You want to locate and understand the irrational or compelling convictions in your mind and decide if that serves YOU, and adjust or drop the belief so you can serve yourself and your happiness.

Viewing your "have tos" or "hate tos" as choices brings a sense of freedom. A simple example would be saying, "I have to get the kids from school." Someone doesn't truly *have to* pick up their children from school; it is a choice, and what probably lies beneath that choice is that your children's safety, wellbeing, and education are important to you. You don't *have to* pick up your kids from school; you *choose to*, because you love them.

Give up your beliefs and limiting thoughts, and let life prove itself to you.

Let Go of Fear

"Unless you are being chased by a scary animal, FEAR is just bad management of your mind."

—Brendon Burchard

The acronym FEAR stands for False Expectations Appearing Real. In fact, most things we fear usually never even happen. Fear is worrying about the future, when you are not in the present moment, but lost in your thoughts of what could happen in the future. Studies show that when people write down their fears for two weeks and predict what will happen, only 85 percent of those predictions actually occur. That is a lot of wasted energy spent worrying about what most likely will just not happen.

Have you ever noticed that when you fear something, you make it out to be way worse in your mind? I learned early on that when I am tired and it's late, if I get my mind spun around a concern, it seems ten times worse than how it turns out to be. My mother called this making a mountain out of a molehill. Colin Powell said, "It ain't as bad as you think. It will look better in the morning." So true! I have a friend with a fear of flying, but she used to travel a few times a year, so she would just muster up the courage and push through the experience. Then came a time in her life where for several years, she wasn't required to travel. The fear grew and when opportunities came up to take a fun trip, she missed out because the fear had become bigger than what she actually remembered experiencing. After many years, she finally took a trip to Hawaii. She had some anxiety prior to and during the flight, but she managed, and it was not nearly as bad as her fear made it out to be for all those years. Does fear ever limit you from experiencing things in life?

About six years ago, I used to golf once a month on average. I initially took lessons to learn the game. I never got good, but I learned how to swing a club and could get through the course. I have wanted to start golfing again for the last year and have had several opportunities, but didn't take advantage of them out of fear of playing badly and being embarrassed on the golf course. I was so afraid of not looking good that I put it off, instead of just going out to have fun. Well, I finally pushed through it and recently went out on the course with a girlfriend from college. I didn't play well, but I had so much fun that it inspired me to start playing again. It was not nearly as bad as I made it out to be all these years. I now actually feel silly for not pursuing the sport again sooner.

The best way to move though fear when it arises is to just *breathe!*

When faced with what scares us, it is natural to hold our breath. It is an attempt to close ourselves off from the fear, but trying to omit fear never works. Start breathing into the fear. Immerse yourself in it. With each inhale, invite the fear in—actually breathe it in. This is how you disarm fear from limiting you, from keeping you from going after and living a life of excitement. There is a very fine line between fear and excitement. It can be crossed with a few deep breaths inviting fear in—not pushing it away or avoiding it. This is how you will gain courage.

Courage does not imply an absence of fear; courage is feeling the fear and saddling up anyway. When you use FEAR as FUEL, it will drive you towards reaching your goals and dreams. Fear is actually a great compass to show you the direction your spirit wants you to go. Use it to determine realistic concerns and decide whether these doubts are even rational. The word "courage" comes from the Latin root word *cour*, which means to tell the story of who you are with your whole heart. In other words, show up in life wholeheartedly. (We'll talk more about this in chapter 5.)

Courage is a muscle you have to build. Do one thing every week that scares you. They can be small things or big things, as long as it's something you want to do but haven't because of fear. It could be fear of trying a new fitness or yoga class, going to dinner or the movies by yourself, or speaking up with your ideas in a meeting. Go for it; push through the fear and build that courage muscle. Before long, the big things you were afraid of will begin to seem small. When you feel the fear and go for it anyway, you will ultimately erase your self-imposed limits and be able to reach your goals and dreams!

Chapter 4

The Power of Authenticity

$\mathcal{C}$hildren come into the world with a deep connection to their spirit and truth. They easily and freely act in alignment with their inner wise voice, or what I call our *native genius*. Unfortunately, unless raised by highly evolved parents, most of us were not taught to foster and honor our native genius. Our loved ones and authority figures, even with the best of intentions and perhaps without realizing it, may have told us repeatedly that we were wrong about what we believed or knew deep down. As children, it didn't take long for us to learn that it was unacceptable to think differently than what we were taught or told to do, and many of us stopped trusting our native genius or even listening to it at all. As a result, rather than easily acting in alignment with our native genius, most of us have layers to our personality, which include the *authentic self*, the *wounded self*, and our *social self*.

Authentic Self vs. Social Self: Why Alignment Is Critical

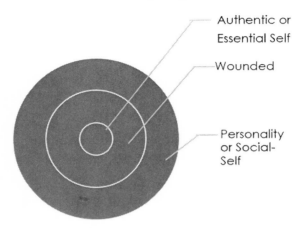

Figure 1. The Layers of Ourselves

The *authentic self* is your soul, spirit, or essential self. It is the truth of who you are, your true essence, and who you came into the world to be. When we live from our authentic self, we show up in the world with vulnerability and the courage to share our whole heart. We align with our deeper wisdom. We embody our truth and then live from our heart center, our core of being. We openly share our passions, unique strengths, and gifts. This enables true connection and the ability to feel alive. Also, when we live from this deep wisdom, we serve others, touch hearts, and make the world a better place. Being your authentic self not only serves you, it serves the world.

Our authentic self speaks to us through a multifaceted language—symbols, music, words, images, and movement—and through this language reveals our native genius. You know you're in alignment with your authentic self when you are participating in anything that allows you to lose all track of time, and when you're done, you can't wait to do it again. It is "getting in the zone," or the place of stillness where your soul can speak to you. It is letting go of the thinking mind and finding silence and stillness within. Any daily practice of silence bears gifts—a heightened sensitivity to beauty, deep inner peace, and a profound feeling of connectedness to all living things. Your passion is way more than an artful expression; it's whatever makes you uniquely you.

The *wounded* self is formed when we experience any level of trauma, mostly during childhood, which contributes to forming the personality. We all have a wounded self, although the degree of woundedness varies. It is caused by any experience we interpret to mean that we are not worthy of love and belonging, or we are not smart enough, pretty enough, or any kind of "enough." It usually happens through criticism, abuse, neglect, misuse of authority, or having to deny or repress ourselves to be accepted. As mentioned above, when told often enough that we are wrong or don't know what we are talking about, we learn to distrust the voice of our authentic self, our native genius, and perhaps stop listening to it entirely.

I remember this happening to me at my father's funeral when I was eight. I was sitting next to my aunt, when I felt my father's spirit come to me and lets me know that all is okay and that I will be fine. When I shared this with my aunt, she looked at me with sympathy, put her hand on my shoulder and said, "Oh honey, that's not possible. You are just overwhelmed with grief." As a child, at my deepest knowing, I remember experiencing my father's presence clearly, yet an authority figure I loved told me not to trust what I knew at the time to be true.

Another example was a knowing I had at age eleven that the man my mother was about to marry was not good for her or us. Up to that point, nothing negative had happened. I had no proof or explanation for what seemed true to me. I just knew, in my heart of hearts, that it was not a good thing. When I expressed this outwardly, I was shut down, told I didn't know what I was talking about, that I was being selfish for not wanting to share my mom, and that I shouldn't want my mom to be alone. As it turned out, this man was a narcissist, and their marriage was full of betrayal and abuse for thirteen years. The emotional turmoil even made my mother physically ill—all because she thought it was more important to hang onto a man and not to be alone than to honor herself.

We all are born with this knowing, this inner voice of wisdom, when we "just know" at our core what is true. But as children, when this ability is wide open, we are often taught to shut it down—or at a minimum we are not encouraged to explore it. These situations teach us to stop trusting our inner wisdom. The good news is that it still dwells within us, and we can begin listening to it again at any time.

The *social self* is formed from both our wounds and the behavior we learn and adopt from our family, culture, religion, upbringing, social positioning, and education. Our social self is what we show to the world, the external face we share, in order to find acceptance, connection, love, and belonging. Unfortunately we often become stuck in our social self, with little or no connection to the authentic self. We live unconsciously, asleep, with no deeper connection to our truth.

Living in the social self alone is living in the shallows of life. In contrast, learning to live from the authentic self is living deeply from your foundation, with purpose, meaning, satisfaction, and joy. When your social self and authentic self are not aligned, you will constantly be searching for something outside of yourself to make you feel okay, worthy, validated, approved, and accepted. This is the endless and constant search of the ego.

Freedom comes from alignment: finding the courage to live authentically, no longer caring what other people think, and instead doing whatever it is that lights you up. Alignment means living with passion and purpose, without the prison walls of conformity. Natural authority is embracing who you are meant to be. Natural authority means living from your core being, your true nature or authentic self, and it is always your greatest place of strength.

A beautiful example of coming into alignment with the authentic self can be best demonstrated with a story from my daughter. Andrea came into the world as an animal advocate and lover. From as early as I can remember, she gravitated to all animals and had a connection with them. She was not yet three years old when Trevor, her brother, was born. As it is common for young toddlers to mimic their mother feeding the new baby with their own baby dolls, my daughter followed suit with one exception. When I would sit down to nurse my son, she would snuggle in a stuffed monkey or dog, lift her shirt, and place it up to her tiny nipple—though she had many baby dolls. I found this quite amusing, but it really told me that nurturing animals came naturally to her.

At about age eight or nine, Andrea began riding American Saddlebred horses and competing in horse shows. These are large horses, highly trained, very high-strung, and sensitive. The average cost of a horse in her competitive category was anywhere from $25,000 to $50,000. She had a natural connection with them, as if she spoke their language. She was never intimidated even when standing on the ground next to them, whether grooming or tacking these large animals. Becoming a good rider was natural for her, too. There was no doubt that her authentic self was coming through with her passion. She was in her glory when she was with those horses.

As she became a young teenager and peer pressure began, she clung to riding even more, as she felt it was the only thing she did well. She saw her friends as great athletes and dancers, therefore she needed something to validate herself as well. So riding gave her a sense of self-worth and belonging. Andrea's social self really enjoyed the accolades she received by winning ribbons and being center stage in the ring.

Around age fourteen or fifteen, a few situations transpired that began to diminish her desire to ride. She was struggling with the choice to continue riding as an expression of her social self, because she was discovering it was not in alignment with her inner knowing, her authentic self. The following excerpt was written by Andrea when she was twenty-three. I wanted to capture her true expression in order to demonstrate the power of alignment.

I think subconsciously I always thought there was something strange about the way the horses were treated, but I was too young to articulate it. The woman who owned the stables and academy where I took riding lessons and leased horses trained her horses by using what is called a "W lunge." It was a system of elastic bands and ropes controlled by the trainer that created tension felt by the horses in order to encourage the horse to lift their hooves higher, thus creating the high-stepping motion characteristic of American Saddlebred horses. This training method was considered to be the most humane. Some trainers use weights, chains, and other mechanisms in order to manipulate the horse's natural form to please the human aesthetic standards for the animal. We used to have a horse that had terrible scars on her lower front legs that were the product of burns from pain-relieving muscle gel. It was put on her legs and then wrapped to create a tingling sensation that encouraged her to pick up her feet. However, the trainer left it on for too long and it irritated and burned her skin, leaving blisters that turned to scars.

A few defining moments for me in realizing that I no longer wanted to participate in showing horses occurred probably ten years ago. Several kids who were at the barn for riding lessons were petting a horse that leaned her head out of her stall. She was the most lovable, friendly horse I think I've ever met. She probably would have curled up in your lap like a dog if she were small enough. While all the kids loved on her, I overheard the woman who owned her (and the property) say the words, "...and that's why that horse is totally useless to us; she's a pet now. She's not a show horse." The woman was so incredibly blind and disconnected to the fact that she regarded another living being purely as a commodity, whose existence was solely for the purpose of her profit or pleasure.

A few months later I went to a week-long riding intensive workshop in Lexington, Kentucky, for other riders my age. A world-renowned auction occurs here where show horses are bought and sold. Watching this horse auction was like witnessing a sort of slave auction: living beings being bought and sold against their will, paraded in front of eager buyers as an auctioneer shouted, like they were simply non-living commodities.

Andrea stopped riding, even though she missed these horses greatly and missed the external validation from her accomplishments. I am not only proud of her, but I admire her ability to be so clear about her authentic self at such a young age, and to be unwilling to live out of alignment with her core truth. She could have easily suppressed or ignored her authentic self's discomfort with the treatment of these horses and allowed her ego and social self only to be satisfied. This is would be an example of non-alignment between the authentic and social self—continuing a behavior even when it does not respect your deeper truth or what is right for you. There is a cost to not living authentically, and it shows up by compromising the depth in which you experience life, your passion, and the ability to love and be inspired. Most importantly, when you don't live in alignment with your truth, there is no way to ever feel good about yourself from the inside out, which is the only place real and lasting validation comes from. Alignment means learning to accept your behavior so completely that it doesn't matter what others think. The authentic self provides the center and strength to do so.

Opportunities to align our social self with our authentic self happen every day. I realized this when Andrea was in kindergarten. She came out of her room one morning, beaming and dressed for school. Her clothes did not match. As a mother, I saw an opportunity to teach her how to pick out her own clothes and match them properly. What would people think of me, as a mother, if I sent my child to school in mismatched clothing? People may think I was a neglectful mother, not even bothering to make sure my child was dressed appropriately for school. I was operating from my social self, concerned with what others would think.

I told Andrea, "Honey, your butterfly skirt doesn't go with your flowered shirt. Please go back to your room and either put on a solid-colored skirt or a solid shirt." My five-year-old replied, "But Mother, butterflies and flowers go beautifully together!" Seriously, how do I argue with that? Especially when her little authentic self was tickled pink with her clothing selection. I was the one trying to limit her authentic expression from *my* social self. I let it go, but it was not an easy thing for me to do at the time. Today, I would have probably never said a word to her in the first place.

When you have the vulnerability and courage to share your authentic self, you are able to access your personal power. How? When you come from your authentic-self:

1. You align with your deeper wisdom.
2. You embody your truth.
3. You live from your heart center—your core of being.
4. You openly share your passions, unique strengths, and gifts.
5. You are always in your greatest place of power when coming from your core or authenticity. Think of it as your sturdy foundation.

Living from your authentic self is the expression of your native genius. It is how you affect the world for the greater good—yours and others'.

Ask yourself: where have I created this alignment in my work and relationships, and where have I not? Remember, when your social self is not in alignment with your authentic self, you're living in the shallows, or the surface of life, where no deep satisfaction can be experienced.

Awakening Provoked: The Ring of Fire

"And the day came when the risk to remain tight in a bud was more painful than the risk it took to blossom."

—Anais Nin

Sometimes we choose to enter this journey to alignment consciously, and sometimes we find ourself on the journey without even knowing we have chosen the path. I recommend you rock your own foundation before it rocks you.

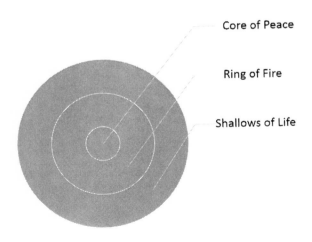

Core of Peace

Ring of Fire

Shallows of Life

Figure 2. Ring of Fire

Figure 2 is another way to illustrate our layers of personality, but this time through the lens of healing. The journey of moving from the *shallows* of life (our social self) in order to live from our *core of peace* (our authentic self) happens by moving through the *ring of fire* (our wounded self). Figure 2 is the clearest and most articulate illustration of this process I have ever found. It is adapted from Martha Beck's book, *Steering by Starlight*. Though I understood this concept itself for years, there was something about this visual that gave me real understanding.

Most people spend their lives avoiding entry into the *ring of fire*, or the pain and uncomfortable feelings of life that exploit our wounds. Instead, many of us usually do whatever it takes to stay on the surface of life, or the *shallows*. The shallows is the place in life where no real depth is experienced and little satisfaction is felt. You can't selectively choose to deeply experience wonderful feelings if you are avoiding the not-so-comfortable feelings. Remember, when we choose to numb out feelings and emotions, we numb out all of them, good and bad. In the shallows, we stay focused on the external aspects of life, the material things, and we judge people around us without introspection. We focus on any distraction we can think of: chasing a better job, buying a bigger house, creating a fatter bank account, shopping, social engagements, alcohol, drugs, sex, working constantly, obsessive fitness, overall nonstop busyness, creating and focusing on the dramas in life, etc. These things help us avoid the pull of the ring of fire. We stay as busy as possible in the shallows, distracting ourselves from any internal dialogue and beliefs that may create discomfort and avoiding the painful emotions that come from our lack of self-love, self-actualization, and self-worth.

Some people manage to live this way their entire life. The result is a shallow, meaningless, and non-purpose-driven existence. They cannot acknowledge or experience the pure joy and purpose of their true nature, and therefore cannot live a meaningful and purposeful life with love, from love. By "love," I don't mean personal love. I mean love on a global, economic, political, and societal level. In our culture, we tend to define "love" as only personal—we love our spouse, our children, or our family. But love is a much wider movement, action, and state of being, and it only has one opposite—fear. Every choice we make in life comes from either fear or love. It is that definitive. So, you are either in a place of fear or in a place of love with the world, the people around you, and yourself. You can't be experiencing real love from a place of fear; they are polar opposites. You can experience feelings of attachment and need, which are based in fear, not love.

Fear of experiencing discomfort from painful feelings and emotions creates a life devoid of love. There is an underlying "something" that is always nagging at us somehow, somewhere. It is often an undistinguished yearning we desperately attempt to fulfill through things outside of us: something from another person, material wealth, our looks, or just attempts to numb out the need. If you are lucky enough to have a life experience force you into the ring of fire from the outside edges of surface existence, there is no turning back— unless you decide to live your life heavily medicated or become a heavy drinker. From everything I've read, our society seems to be experiencing addiction, obesity, debt, and depression at the highest rate in history. We continually look outside ourselves for relief when we bump up against the ring of fire, instead of journeying through the ring of fire to find our *core of peace*. No final answer or satiety of peace can be found except within our own hearts and soul.

On the other hand, some circumstances may warrant psychiatric drugs to be able to continue the journey. When someone simply cannot emerge from the darkness, then an antidepressant may be a necessary but temporary aid, in conjunction with psychotherapy and spiritual guidance. But it shouldn't be a way of life. All too often, drugs are used as a crutch to avoid the ring of fire instead of doing the work to get through it. We want the quick fix; we want to take a pill and have everything be okay without doing our work. But there is no way through any pain or discomfort without first going in.

Navigating through the Ring of Fire

I have had my own personal experience with antidepressants. I was thirty-three, living the American dream with a husband who was a good man and provider, two cars and a boat that were paid for, money in the bank, a beautiful home, and two healthy children—one boy and one girl. Yet, even though I had achieved all the external circumstances we are taught will make us happy,

I was miserable. We are so conditioned to believe that once we achieve the "American dream" and all the external signs of success, all will be great and we will be happy. The depression set in when I realized I had achieved all this, yet I still wasn't happy. At the time, I was a stay-at-home mom. I took an antidepressant for a year to tolerate my feelings of hopelessness. It numbed me out just enough so that I didn't experience the depth of discomfort I needed to take action or make changes in my life, specifically to nurture my soul and face the truth that was lurking at the depths. It was simply an attempt to stay in the *shallows* and not enter the *ring of fire*.

At age thirty-four, I went back to work after five years at home. I was out in the world again, earning a living, and gaining some confidence back, and I was able to wean myself off the antidepressant. Having taken the drug for a year, I felt it was important to not become dependent on it. Taking control of my life and re-entering the workforce gave me enough motivation and lift to realize that taking anything long term wasn't a valid solution. Little did I know that I was about to enter the *ring of fire* full force.

I finally began to face the truth behind why I had felt so miserable, and what drove me to take the antidepressant in the first place; I was experiencing no passion or intimacy with my husband. It felt like an arranged marriage. It was easy for me to ignore this for a while as a stay-at-home mom, with all of my energy going towards two small children. But I was starved for passion and needed to feel alive, which was definitely related to my depression and lack of connection to my own spirit.

I know now that depression signifies a lack of connection to your soul and the presence of negative thought patterns that are preventing you from believing in yourself and your worth. Depression means you are not honoring yourself or your life, and you are not tuned into the stillness and present moment where your soul, God, or spirit can be heard. In short, depression is a sign that you are not living from your authentic self.

As I began to face the truth about my marriage and began my search to find passion and feel alive again, I didn't realize at the time that what I was ultimately searching for was my authentic self, my core of peace. I still believed happiness would be found through a man.

As I attended conferences all over the United States, I started having a crazy urge to have an affair, especially after I realized other males found me attractive. I was working for a technology manufacturer based in southern California, and about six months in, I went to the headquarters for a week of meetings. I had an affair with Bill, a work colleague. It was electrical and magnetic, like nothing I had ever experienced before, and something I was so starved for. The last time I can remember that intensity was after my first makeout session as a young teen. I had felt different afterwards; it was my first experience with sexual desire and lust. This affair felt very similar. It became my new antidepressant, or drug.

When I returned home to my husband and children in Tampa, it was clear that I had crossed a line of integrity and had no interest or desire to stay in my marriage. In fact, that first weekend was excruciating for me. I distinctly remember wondering that weekend how anyone could cheat and then go home to their spouse and children and act as nothing had happened. Living in the corporate world and traveling regularly, I realized many people actually do live this way. I have met many married men in business who claimed to love their wives while attempting to seduce me.

One thing was for sure—after that hot week in California, I wanted my freedom. Passion (although unhealthy) was alive in me again. I announced to my husband that I would be finding an apartment and would be out within a month. It didn't come as a surprise to him; we had come close to separating many times. But now I had real motivation, even if it was misguided, and it got me to move forward with a change I needed to make. My only regret is that I didn't find the courage to leave my marriage without the affair and that I had compromised my integrity to find the courage to leave. I never looked back or second-guessed my decision to divorce. I did grieve deeply for breaking up the family unit; there was no way to ever recover that pure nucleus again. I did make desperate attempts to recreate the "family" circle. But the fact that I was desperate was exactly why I was unable to recreate a family with a man again.

Coming from a desperate place always keeps our desires at bay. Instead, the desperation, which is rooted in fear (not love), pulls in exactly what you don't want. When we are attached to having anything, that attachment energetically won't allow it to come in. When we are clear with our intention, put that intention out to the universe or God to fulfill, and then let go, knowing that we will be okay with or without it, and it will magically show up in our life.

I was obviously not very evolved at this point in my life. I was simply trying to feel good, and I was attempting to make Bill my feel-good drug. I tried to jump straight from my marriage into a relationship with him. To say it was rocky would be putting it mildly—what I was about to experience over the next three years was excruciating.

Though I didn't know it at the time, my relationship with Bill was the defining moment of my entrance into my own *ring of fire*. It was the catalyst that allowed me to make the necessary changes I needed in my life to begin my journey down the spiritual path of finding self-love. Bill opened the door to my journey (well, it was more like a blast through a gun barrel) from the shallows to the ring of fire. Unfortunately, I did not see the affair as a catalyst that was supposed to spark self-discovery and being on my own, so I clung to an unhealthy, dysfunctional relationship with a man who was not capable of being emotionally present with me. And truth be told, we were a perfect match at the time. His inability to be emotionally available to me was equal to my inability to be emotionally available to myself. The relationship was a rollercoaster of the lowest lows and the highest highs, just like a drug. My desperateness to make the relationship work, believing it was the answer to ending my pain, started a cadence of psychotherapy and couples' counseling. This provided brand-new insight for me. I began to realize that I had huge control issues due to my fear of being abandoned. Bill's emotional abandonment was the reflection of my wounds that needed to be brought to the surface so I could heal them. At the time, I was focused on changing him, a misguided attempt to feel safe within myself. In my unconscious place, I believed that if I could get him to be emotionally available, then I would be okay. But in actuality, I was responsible for learning to be there for myself. It was a few years later before I was really capable of seeing this clearly.

Bill was no doubt a soulmate; his soul contract was to shake me up to the point that I could grow and evolve. Most people believe we have one soulmate and this person will be the love of our life. I disagree. I believe we have many soulmates, and soul contracts, in a lifetime. Soul contracts are agreements we make at a soul level before our birth into the physical world. These soul contracts bring soulmates together in situations that affect us deeply and provide the lessons needed to hopefully shift and evolve to something greater than simply living in our own thoughts and in the material world. We are all here to help one another reconnect with our authentic selves. Soulmates are meant to stir you up, shake you to the core, and bring you to your knees, so you have no choice but to look for the answers that will lead you home. Soulmates aren't necessarily the person you are meant to spend your life with in harmony, but they can be. The point is to reconnect with the divine perfection or essence that is within all of us.

Before Bill, I had always picked men that were beneath me in intellect, education, and overall self-esteem. I was miserable and didn't respect them, but I was safe, as they were not going to leave me. Bill was the first man that I ever allowed myself to be vulnerable with, but the attachment I had to him was so very unhealthy. I did not know who I was without him. Shortly after our relationship began, I started an amazing and lucrative position for Cisco Systems. Remember, I had a completely opposite personality in the business world than I did in my personal relationships. Most people would have been shocked to know that the kickass account manager would curl up on the floor of her walk-in closet in the fetal position, feeling total fear, as if she was going to die over losing some guy. Usually this immobilization happened after an argument; Bill would leave and sometimes not speak to me for a week after an argument. It was emotionally devastating. Being abandoned with no resolution deeply triggered my childhood wounds. I knew it made no logical or intellectual sense that I felt as if my physical survival was at stake, but that is truly how terrified I felt at the time. I was reliving a childhood trauma.

The relationship with Bill ended permanently after three full years of recycling the same drama and pain. He ended it, thank God, because I was never able to pull the plug—even though I wanted out and knew it was becoming physically unhealthy for me; I was exhausted and life in general was becoming a struggle. I then spent an entire year of doing everything I could to heal, or at least I thought I was at the time. I went to therapy, read lots of great spiritual and self-help books, attended many personal development seminars, stopped drinking any alcohol, and took great care of myself physically with a great diet and lots of exercise. But I was in so much pain that I could easily get upset just by seeing a car that looked like his on the road. My suffering was immense; I felt unbearable anxiety at times. I would wake up in the middle of the night completely panicked and could not logically understand why. Instead of reliving my childhood trauma only some of the time, I was now reliving it constantly.

I was still completely emotionally attached, and I wanted the relationship back; it was an addiction. I developed a whole new empathetic understanding for drug addicts. I knew exactly what the withdrawal and cravings must have felt like. I was white-knuckling through my own kind of sobriety. I realized addiction was addiction, and you can be addicted to a person or relationship just like drugs or alcohol. You are looking for something external to make you feel good, and the price of those constant temporary feel-goods you get from any type of addiction can be fatal. At a minimum, until you learn to find your feel-good from within through the development of your own self-love, your quality of life can only be that of merely existing. You'll either be stuck in constant "search mode," or remain numb and unconscious. You will never fully thrive and have a fulfilling life when you look for happiness externally.

Looking back, I realize that I was viewing this relationship as a means to my self-worth. If he wouldn't change for me, that meant there was something wrong with me. This was a huge aha moment for me. I made someone else's behavior a factor in my worth. I had been so consumed with changing *him*, and in the process I gave away my power to him when he didn't even know it or want it.

The very first self-help book I read was *In the Meantime* by Iyanla VanZant. It was after my breakup with Bill. The book focused on the misbelief that a woman's self-worth directly correlates to being loved by a man. VanZant used an analogy of a three-story home, with a basement, to illustrate our levels of consciousness, with the "attic " symbolizing the woman who had achieved self-actualization or enlightenment and the basement symbolizing you were unconscious. I quickly became aware, according to her book, that I was a "basement dweller"—in essence, asleep on myself. It was earth-shattering to realize that my unconscious thought ran rampant in my life, and I didn't even know it. I was purely a reactionary creature, constantly searching for some form of external feel-good—usually a man to love me. I also realized for the first time that many other women operated and felt the same way I did. We all have a story we tell ourselves—about ourselves. Telling ourselves that anyone or anything from our past has power over us and defines us or our worth is the biggest fattest lie we could ever subject ourselves to.

This period of my life was the hardest and yet most necessary on my path to learning self-love. It took two more dysfunctional relationships after Bill to really understand the lesson and to transcend my old story completely—specifically, that I was not as good as other people without a man. If I had spent even half the effort on becoming whole within that I had spent on fixing, supporting, and trying to change the guy in my life, my journey would have been shorter and less painful. If I had known better, I would have done better. We learn, heal, and let go in layers; we all get it when we get it and not a moment sooner.

The concept I needed to learn was that I needed to shift my thoughts from others to myself. My first helpful therapist, Patricia Noll, whose practice was appropriately named Focus One, told me repeatedly that I had to get the focus off the other person and back on me. But it took years before that "aha" truly happened for me.

But even once I began to understand why I behaved the way I did, I still didn't know how to fix or change it. I was still very attached to wanting what I wanted. I still wanted to change the relationship to be what I wanted, instead of acknowledging that it didn't work for me and letting go, and most importantly—I was the one that needed to change. Even though I was wounded with abandonment issues, I was also sort of a spoiled brat, used to getting my way as a child if I put up a big enough fight. In other words, I was more focused on getting my way than I was on finding peace—because I believed getting what I wanted would bring me peace and happiness. I hadn't learned that I am solely responsible for my peace, and that the source of that peace was within. As the saying goes, "Would you rather be right, or happy?"

So even though I intellectually understood the importance of getting the focus on me, the real work and journey was moving the concept from my head to my heart and then really practicing and applying it to my everyday life. I made the mistake of believing that because I understood spiritual truths on an intellectual basis, I had mastered it. Just because I could recite it didn't mean I got it—quite the opposite. In fact, I wonder if our intellectual understanding actually slows down our mastery of spiritual truths, or if it is a necessary first step to getting there. I believe there are three layers of learning: first we become aware, then we understand (with the intellect/ego), and then there is the true knowing. True knowing comes from within, a sort of core encapsulation within our heart that we can then live from, it is a deep sense of knowing

One year after the breakup, I met Jill, a psychotherapist by training who was also a spiritual healer or guide. It was Jill's work that finally allowed me to fully embrace these concepts at the heart level and be able to put them into practice. I would put the energetic healing she offers in the same category of shamans and energy workers, but because of her therapy background, she brings another layer of understanding to the process and a bridge for those who come from a more conventional perspective.

Her gift was to "hold space" for healing, to take others into a deep meditative place, where there was no concept of time. We didn't spend hours rehashing my past, my family, and my relationships. Instead, we would begin each session by focusing on my intent and talking about what I wanted to get out of the session. Then we would get still and meditate. Jill would verbally walk me through a visual process that ultimately led me to greater union within myself. The disassociated parts of myself, resulting from trauma in earlier life experiences, had created a separation between my soul and my moment-to-moment existence. Jill's healing process reintegrated these dissociated parts with the truth of my divine being. I learned from Jill that the purpose of healing was to chip away the layers of our social self, or external personality, to reclaim our divine inner nature, which is pure love. The result was a sense of wholeness, and the ability to experience joy, which is our God-given birthright.

After my first two-hour session with her, I had completely disconnected emotionally from Bill. It felt miraculous! He was still in my thoughts occasionally, but there was no emotional charge whatsoever; it was neutral. Jill said she literally saw a cord of connection between us dissolve, and that she had never experienced anything like that with anyone else. (I believe it was because he was a soulmate; it was a powerful connection.) Jill's gift to me was the guidance she provided through my ring of fire.

After I had become disconnected from Bill, one wonderful side effect was that I clearly saw the good in our past relationship, rather than just desperation and heartache. I realized that Bill and I had a lot of fun and laughter. He was easygoing, which was a nice balance for my intense type-A personality. He is also responsible for helping me fully embrace my sexuality at age thirty-four. He was always complimentary; I felt physically adored and never self-conscious of my body. After seeing Jill one day, I remember driving home in my convertible and looked up at the sky. I saw the most amazing sunrays streaking through the clouds, as if heaven itself was shining down on me. Then, as if in a dream, I saw Bill's face. With a nod and smile, he affirmed, "You got the lesson you were meant to get from me; you got yourself." He was a huge pivotal point in my life, and I am grateful for my awakening through our experience together—although I'm also happy it is behind me and I never will be there again!

Over the years, through the lens of my own experience, I began to notice many other powerful businesswomen were giving themselves away in romantic relationships. They had a strong sense of self-worth professionally, but barely any when it came to men. As I've learned to become more authentic and to champion and honor myself in personal relationships, the business side of me has actually softened. The imbalance has evened out as I have learned to love myself. Of course, I am continually learning and expanding, and I believe I will do so my whole life.

The Only Way Out Is In

Instead of waking up and heading into my ring of fire, I could have easily stayed where I was—married, taking an antidepressant, and being comfortably numb. Like I mentioned earlier, the take-a-pill, quick-fix mentality helps us avoid our authentic self, at the cost of living life without much feeling or joy.

But this society of "comfortable numbness" is preventing the evolution of our species. We need to wake up! The only way to joy and happiness is to go from the shallow edges right through the middle, into the pain that will lead you back to your truth, your authentic self, or your soul. The only way out is in.

If you're ready to move out of the shallows and face your ring of fire, I have just one piece of advice for you: Welcome discomfort when it shows up. Here's how:

1. **Don't armor up.** Don't say you're okay when you're not. We force a smile when we don't feel like it. We pretend to enjoy things we don't. Pretending we're fine when we aren't is like suffocating ourselves. It keeps us from getting what we need most at times of grief—a connection to our feelings, our soul, and people in our lives we can lean on.

2. **Invite the pain in and sit with it.** I know this sounds counterintuitive, but I mean this with all my heart. There is no quicker way to disarm and dissipate pain than to let it in. So often when we feel sad or anxious, we work hard to stuff or avoid the feeling. Feelings are an internal experience, while emotions are the outward expression of our feelings. Just as a duck or a dog will shake off tension, we too have to release feelings through healthy outwardly expressed emotions. Sometimes just letting the outward expression or emotion come out is all that is needed to move past uncomfortable feelings.

Give yourself permission to feel your feelings, and express your emotions in a big way, whatever they may be. Cry, if you want—cry hard, express the feeling outward.

When I grieve any loss in my life, I invite the pain in by telling myself, "I can handle this," or "It is just an experience, it is not permanent, and the more quickly I allow the feeling to emerge, the more quickly it will pass." When I let my feelings freely bubble to the surface and allow an emotional outward response, the negative feelings of sadness or anxiety then pass quickly. It starts with getting in touch with what you are feeling, paying attention to your feelings, as opposed to subconsciously repressing feelings of discomfort. When you allow feelings to expand, they shrink and pass quickly.

Even though the sun cannot be seen on a rainy day, it is always there, waiting for us behind the clouds. The same is true for your authentic self, your native genius. It's still there, beneath your wounds, your upbringing, and your defense mechanisms. The ring of fire is what will burn away the clouds so your authentic self can emerge in all its glory—and the only way forward is travel through it.

Traveling through the ring of fire will almost certainly make you feel vulnerable and at risk. But as we'll learn in the next chapter, vulnerability is nothing to be feared; it is the path to freedom.

Chapter 5

Vulnerability: The Path of the Free

"Dance like no one is watching. Sing like no one is listening. Love like you've never been hurt and live like it's heaven on Earth."

—Mark Twain

raveling through the ring of fire requires us to become *vulnerable.* The trouble is that most of us believe that vulnerability should be avoided at all costs. If asked what the word *vulnerability* means, most people would say it is a sign of weakness, a negative and undesirable trait. As for me, I was taught that I needed to protect myself from becoming vulnerable. Vulnerability meant I was putting myself at risk and exposing myself to being hurt, which was certainly something I didn't want. It takes courage to be vulnerable; in fact, I think the terms are almost interchangeable. As we learned earlier, the word *courage* comes from the Latin root word *cour*, or heart. There is nothing weak about being courageous, or living from your heart; therefore, being vulnerable is not weak.

The truth is that vulnerability is the birthplace for *all* feelings and emotions. Why? Because we cannot say, "I want to be vulnerable enough to feel love, joy, and deep connection to others, but I want to avoid all hurt, disappointment, and rejection." Again, you cannot selectively choose what you are vulnerable to; you are either opening your heart to new experiences, or you aren't. Most of us want the ability to feel deep love and joy, but may not even realize that by avoiding vulnerability, we are limiting the degree to which we experience these positive emotions. If you want to feel positive emotions, you have to be open to the possibility of the not-so-pleasant ones, too. This groundbreaking research by Brené Brown, cited earlier,[8] can truly help change the way we live and show up in our lives.

Figure 3. Vulnerability Is the Birthplace of All Emotions

There is, however, a filter you can apply to vulnerability: *thick skin, big heart.* It means you don't take the uncomfortable or painful experiences personally as if they determine your self-worth. You keep your heart open and allow the bad to wash right through you. Don Miguel Ruiz did a great job of explaining this in his book *The Four Agreements*. If you don't take anything personally, you can always keep your heart open to experience love and joy without letting the uncomfortable emotions define you.

Vulnerability is, in fact, the only way to be truly safe. When your sense of peace and worthiness is no longer dependent on what others think or say, then you are safe within, no matter what happens around or outside of you. We become willing to allow ourselves be deeply seen, rather than controlling and predicting our environment for safety out of fear.

So I believe true vulnerability is the opposite of weakness. When we have the courage to reveal our whole heart, we have chosen the path of authenticity and freedom. Our self-created prison walls dissolve when we give up caring about what other people think of us, and we are free to be ourselves, to show up with our whole heart, to live a life of true creativity, innovation, and joy.

Vulnerability in the Workplace

Vulnerability in the corporate environment is often difficult to find. But if vulnerability is the birthplace of creativity, and creativity drives innovation, then how successful can any corporation be long-term if it is not safe for people to be vulnerable enough to brainstorm, share ideas, take risks, and make mistakes? If people feel shame from the fear of ridicule or making a mistake, they will eventually disengage. From there, you are left with a culture of only process and function. Also, in a culture of blame and shame, when finger pointing is prevalent and no one wants to take responsibility for their mistakes, there is no real accountability, and therefore no real innovation or change. Definitely no passion.

People have to feel comfortable being creative and trying new things, and it needs to be acceptable to fail. Some companies actually have a requirement to fail and to fail often. The foundational philosophy is that if you are not failing often, then you are not being creative enough in thinking up new ideas. How fun would it be to work for a company like that? I highly recommend checking out Zappos.com and their company culture. You can learn more about their amazing and leading edge culture at www.deliveringhappiness.com.

Consider some of our greatest inventors. They all tried and tried again, countless times, before finally developing some of the greatest inventions in modern history. Einstein and Thomas Edison are examples of vulnerability and resilience. Everyone would benefit from not viewing failure as a negative concept, but as synonymous with the persistent creativity that drives change and innovation. There are always great lessons to be learned when a situation doesn't go as wanted or planned. This had been a huge lesson for me, as I was raised in a family where mistakes were frowned upon and not usually acceptable.

I worked for a Fortune 500 company many years ago that began to shift to a culture of blame, shame, finger pointing, and a lack of accountability. Shortly after they went public and Wall Street became their driving force, this negative culture really solidified. There was, and still is, no longer any room for creativity or innovation. In fact, I recently heard that a senior executive held a company meeting where he ranted at, yelled at, belittled, and threatened employees. I don't need to be an organizational psychologist to know that a message of "the beatings will continue until morale improves" will not impart creativity, passion, and motivation from employees. In fact, it will create the exact opposite—disengagement. What is most needed in this situation (and others like it) is leadership that will positively motivate and encourage employees to be creative, which will create buy-in to the company's mission and vision. A great leader appeals to the emotions of an employee to gain their trust, enable creativity, and spark passion to drive change, innovation, and success.

Let's say you do have to face a hostile company culture each day. Can you armor up at work and then take it off at home? I would have to say no. It takes a lot of work to show up every day in protection mode, and over time, it will become a pattern or habit. You can't walk in the front door in the evening to your family and easily peel back the armor. You are one person— switching personas will become impossible, or at least way too much work. Again, when we don't share our vulnerability in one area, we most likely will not show vulnerability in any area. You are either a person that demonstrates vulnerability or not.

What Keeps Us from Being Vulnerable?

What usually gets in the way of being vulnerable and sharing our truth is *a lack of self-worth*, and then defining ourselves by our self-worth according to others' approval and acceptance. This was my biggest barrier, for sure. Even after a fifteen-year journey of self-discovery and self-love, it still takes conscious effort to remember my truth and not to try to conform in an attempt to fit in, especially in the corporate world. I often don't feel as though I fit in at places like Cisco, especially when I show up authentically, but that is okay. It is a very cerebral environment, and though I am bright, I am anything but intellectual, which is what this culture values. I continually have to validate myself and remind myself that it is okay not to be intellectual, because I am bringing a different perspective to the conversation. I am focused on people, connecting, and driving the conversation to a deeper level. I often am the one that re-humanizes the culture. The corporate world needs more connections and value placed on human beings. I have value; it just may not be the type of value most are competing for within the corporate culture. I am certain there are times when people are rolling their eyes at me or thinking I am unintelligent. I now say, "Who cares!" because maybe, just maybe, I am giving someone else permission to offer up their truth and change the conversation from conformity to connection.

What's Enough?

As a result of our lack of inner self-worth, we have become a culture of "never enough." Why? We are looking to find self-worth through *having* rather than being, as if more power, money, and material possessions will fill the void created by a lack of deep connection to ourselves and to others. But why can't being loving and kind and living a good life be enough? We are obsessed with being special and standing out, as if we all have to reach celebrity status to be good enough. There is a belief that approval and acceptance happens by seeming extraordinary—and we need outside validation to prove it. Facebook is a perfect example, with people sharing every detail of their life in an attempt to make themself appear important, instead of simply showing up and *living* life. Look at the success of (and our obsession with) reality TV. I recently heard that Snooki was the honoree at the Rutgers University commencement. Really? If that doesn't make a huge statement about what's important in our world, nothing will. If being a celebrity truly was the end-all, be-all to having enough, then we'd expect celebrities to be thriving role models. Yet, we constantly hear about celebrity drug addictions, alcohol problems, abuse, weight problems, and horrific breakups. Clearly, fame and wealth are not enough either.

This particular point hit home for me during a 2012 Oprah interview with Whitney Houston. This was Whitney's first and only interview after she had supposedly become clean from drugs. She recounted her relationship with Bobby Brown and how they would go two weeks at a time just sitting in front of the television smoking pot laced with rock cocaine and literally not speak to one another except for an occasional nod and half-assed laugh. She spoke of the emotional abuse and cheating she accepted from him. What flabbergasted me, and what I couldn't stop thinking, was this: Here is one of the most absolutely beautiful, successful, and talented women in the world, and yet she still didn't feel good enough. If she had loved and valued herself, there is no way her relationship with Bobby would have lasted as long as it did. So, even though she *had* enough, it still wasn't enough to bring her joy and freedom in the absence of self-love. Lack of self-love and self-worth is the only reason any woman would put up with someone like Bobby Brown and never fully recover.

However, her story hits very close to home for me, and I am certain for many other women as well. I have never experienced stardom or been involved in recreational drugs, but I have been addicted—to men and relationships. Whitney even said in the interview that Bobby was her drug. "The guy was my drug" is a clear-cut statement that she had no self-esteem in the relationship. Whitney may have gotten clean for a while, but she obviously never truly healed or developed self-love, and therefore was drawn back to the addiction. Her story hit me like a ton of bricks—that could have been me at one point in my life, because my self-worth was totally wrapped up in having a man, any man, by my side.

Waking up to "I'm good enough" was my turning point of freedom. I realized that loving myself is the foundation to feeling good enough. Special love or romantic love can be so deceiving, like it is our savior. I have read countless stories about people that have had the most excruciating hardships in life, but when asked about their pain, they recount stories about romantic heartbreak—just like the Cambodian refugees I mentioned in the Introduction. Heartbreak is one of the primary illusions driving the human species to continually seek worthiness through another instead of finding their internal path to wholeheartedness, joy, and love. Someone once told me that you could take *any* love song and redirect as if you were singing it to God, your own spirit or soul, and it would make so much more sense, because that is always your primary love relationship. Give it some thought next time you hear a love song.

Isn't love the most important and desired human experience? Only a sociopath would say they would be willing to never experience love again. Experiencing love is a direct reflection of our love for ourselves—not just romantic love, but in all contexts. But we don't we talk about it! We have made the word "love" taboo outside of our personal relationships—at work, in our non-romantic relationships, in politics, and in our communities. Isn't that what the world needs—more love? Isn't that what makes the world go round? We have all heard it a thousand times, yet we don't take it seriously or act accordingly. I know the corporate world needs a *whole lotta love*. For example, Zappos.com lives by the motto PLUR (Peace. Love. Unity. Respect.) How awesome would it be if more corporate cultures incorporated PLUR?

Nevertheless, when I speak to corporate women about the workplace, I am still careful with my use of the word "love." Not because I am not willing to be vulnerable, but because I don't want to turn them off up front. I still have to meet people halfway. So I only use words and phrases like trust, respect, kindness, connection, and allowing yourself to be truly seen– but not *love*. However, after seeing Marianne Williamson use the word *love* in her congressional candidacy platform, I am now questioning whether I too could muster up the courage to use the word *love* in the corporate sector. We need to bring the love back into work! Humanitarian values have to be a part of any company or government's bottom line, not just economic gain, to create sustainability for everyone.

"We can only love others as much as we love ourselves."

I remember the first time I heard this statement from a therapist. I argued it wasn't true. Most parents would claim the same, often saying they love their children more than themselves. But really, being willing to protect your child with your own life is instinctual, and is not reflective of loving your children more than yourself. Regarding someone's life as more than your own doesn't mean you love that person more. I know now, without a doubt, that the degree to which I love myself is the degree to which I can love another, even my own children. To be specific: Our ability to be vulnerable and empathetic with ourselves is equivalent to how vulnerable and empathetic we can be with our own children. When we carry our own shame with us, being judgmental prevails, instead of the ability to be empathic and compassionate.

Looking back, I can see where this happened with my own children before I developed the ability to be loving and compassionate with myself. My daughter would come home crying because someone had been verbally mean to her, didn't let her in their circle of friends, or criticized how she was dressed or looked. I would attempt to brush it off quickly and minimize her feelings; I was not capable of validating her experience with compassion. I had experienced many hurtful situations like this and came home from school crying as a child myself. I was holding onto shame from my own childhood, and becoming empathic to Andrea would require me to reach into my own pain. At the time, I was unable to console her or really allow myself to understand what she was feeling. Instead, I judged her or invalidated her feelings, although I didn't realize what I was doing at the time. Today I make a conscious effort to tune into my own vulnerability so I can feel compassion and empathy for others. After all, feeling empathy gives you the capacity to love.

Unfortunately, studies have shown a decline in empathy over the last twenty years in our society.[9] Some of this is directly due to technology. Think about if a friend sends a text to another friend who is deeply upset over a breakup. It is easy to type words that sound empathetic, but if you are not looking into someone's eyes and sensing how they are truly feeling, they are just pixels on a screen. How empathetic are you really being to that person? You are most likely just going through the motions and saying what is expected. Going through the motions at a distance does not allow people to develop empathy.

Something rather humorous, yet worthy of consideration that I heard Brené Brown mention in one of her lectures, is the effect of Botox on empathy. I know that sounds ridiculous, but think about it. As women are using Botox more and more often to paralyze muscles in their faces, they become less capable of communication through facial expressions. A subtle look can share huge empathy or feeling. Consider how often communication may be completely missed because of lack of expression on a frozen face.

Breaking the "Fitting In" Barrier

When our primary goal in any situation is not about love or empathy, but rather fitting in, we are attempting to seek approval and are not living authentically. Seeking approval is the opposite of accepting ourselves. Most of us are masters at becoming chameleons, assessing and acclimating to any situation in an attempt to fit in. Some people actually pride themselves on being chameleons. But here is the problem with becoming a chameleon—you don't show up authentically by living the truth of who you are and allowing yourself to be truly seen.

Why is that a problem? For starters, your self-worth is put on the line when you attempt to assume the same position or perspective as everyone else. If your chameleon efforts don't produce approval or acceptance, then you will feel worse than ever. Fitting in and seeking approval to belong, instead of accepting ourselves and sharing it with others, keeps us focused on performing, pleasing, and perfecting.

So what's wrong with that? Without the courage to live authentically, we deprive ourselves and others from seeing new perspectives, ideas, and possibilities. In short, we squash creativity. When you don't depend on the approval of others to feel worthy, your self-worth is no longer on the line. The barrier to fitting in is then removed, because conformity is not necessary for self-acceptance. You can share your thoughts and ideas freely.

There is no doubt that the "P" words—performing, pleasing, perfecting—are a big, fat trap for most of us. They become a coat of armor to keep us from being vulnerable, because we seek approval from others as a form of protection. We want to make sure we are liked and approved of in order to feel safe. It is an attempt to keep the attention off ourselves and our own wounds that need empathy, compassion, and acceptance from within. In essence, performing, pleasing, and perfecting keep us from taking responsibility for our own sense of worth; they make us completely addicted and dependent on others to feel good enough.

Speaker and bestselling author Brené Brown lives by a great motto when making choices that could lead to trying to please others—"Seek discomfort over resentment." I have seen many friends deplete themselves on a regular basis because they spend their energy putting others first and saying "yes" when they want to say "no." In most cases, they've been living in the "people pleasing" mode for so long, they don't even know they are doing it. It's the role they learned to play to find approval and acceptance from others or in their family system. They believe it is what they are supposed to be doing.

People that are pleasers see it as their responsibility. But at what cost? I find pleasers are often not particularly trustworthy. I am never sure if they are being authentic or if they will end up being resentful and passive aggressive later. I have watched beautiful and talented girlfriends give themselves away to their spouses and jobs, to the point that they are physically ill—yet they don't see the correlation between their behavior and health. They carry so much unacknowledged and unconscious resentment and anger that it is literally eating them from the inside out. I call it compromising your own happiness to make others believe you are happy.

When you stop people pleasing, many people may be ticked off at first. They won't understand; they are conditioned to get their way with you. So when you change the game on them, there will be some backlash. It is no different than suddenly enforcing a bedtime on a toddler who had been making his own bedtime decisions. There will be pushback and tantrums until the new dynamic settles in. The people you have been pleasing will adjust too; most importantly, they will develop a new respect for you. Don't you respect people more when they tell you "no" with firm, yet gentle boundaries, like saying, "I would really like to help or be there, but I am not going to be able to. Thanks for asking me, and please ask me again"?

I have learned to incorporate "discomfort over resentment" in my relationships, and it works beautifully. It is a little hurdle to jump over at the front end, but it saves so much long-term resentment and drama in relationships, which can become a big hurdle over time. I was recently dating someone, and very early on in the relationship, we regularly split the dinner bill. I realized that I wasn't okay with the fact that he never once told me to put my card away when I offered to pay. I knew with time I would become resentful. So, I decided to choose discomfort over resentment, and brought the issue up in a conversation. I told him that it was uncomfortable to voice my want, but I didn't want to become resentful. I explained that I wanted to be courted, and that I would appreciate it if he would offer to pay for dinner more often. He said, "Sure, no problem, and thank you for sharing your feelings and being open." Enough said! Just put it out there. When we don't share our feelings in the moment to avoid a little bit of discomfort at the front end, we only exchange it for huge discomfort at the back end—in any situation in life.

Choosing discomfort over resentment can also mean saying "yes." Learn to say "yes" to the things you want to do so you don't resent never doing them. How often do you put off your joys because you don't give yourself permission to say "yes" to you? Find a way to say "yes" to that trip you have been wanting to take, going back to school, or trying something new. Honor your desires and let go of excuses; instead, make the commitment to do what it takes to make it happen.

Performing and perfecting are no different—they are about seeking approval from others and not looking inward. All three P's are a form of addiction, a way to keep us afloat, surviving from situation to situation in order to be fulfilled. When that outside validation doesn't happen, our self-worth is devastated and we become victims to not feeling good enough. When our validation is derived from seeking perfection or from our performance, our ability to feel worthy of love and belonging will always be at the mercy of others. Shame and defeat will always be a shadow—stopping you from falling into the divine *you*, worthy of love and belonging without pleasing, perfecting, or performing.

Let go of perfectionism. It's a trap! You are keeping yourself from experiencing life when you focus on doing something perfectly. Perfectionism is not greatness; it is an approval-seeking addiction and limits your creativity and ability to experience joy. Perfectionism is a sure sign that you do not love yourself and value your worth; you're believing in the lie that being perfect is the only way to be okay or good enough in the eyes of others, and it keeps you from focusing on your stuff. How you feel is more important than what other people think.

Perhaps the most obvious place we see evidence of the three P's is in our body image as women. Take a look at our $60 billion beauty industry. I heard a statistic that if every woman in North America stopped buying beauty products for one week, the industry would collapse to the same degree as the airline industry did after 9/11. The most ironic thing about it is that most men don't even like all the makeup—we dress to impress each other. Our society has created unrealistic standards and expectations around body image and appearance, and women uphold them by judging and criticizing other women. We want to "do it all, do it perfectly, and look great while doing it!" Body image and appearance are our biggest source of inadequacy as women. We focus on our external beauty so much, yet if the same effort was focused on developing our internal beauty and shining it outward, our true beauty would be greater than any aesthetics treatment could create. Our real divine feminine beauty comes from our authentic power within, shining outward. The average American girl will have compared bodies with a girlfriend in the mirror by age eight, and by age thirteen, she will have been on at least one diet. I know I personally struggle with how I talk to myself when I get up in the morning and look in the mirror. The voice inside my head can easily say, "Tired, dimply legs, stomach is getting flabby, more lines on my face—and what is up with my hair?" What if we turned that around, and we all endorsed ourselves? "You look great! You take great care of yourself. I love you. Go get 'em!'"

Honoring and supporting ourselves is key. How we treat ourselves is the most important thing in learning self-love, which can only happen by being vulnerable, letting go of shame, and living with an open heart. Only when we embody these things can we connect to our true creative and loving energy.

The Recipe for Creativity: Rest and Play

Myth: The more hardworking and exhausted you are, the more you should feel validated, be successful and a have greater sense of self-importance.

Truth: We falsely define ourselves by what we do for a living and accomplish in the world, not by who we are and what we love. This is normal in the United States, but not everywhere else.

I was raised by a mother who was taught that being lazy was shameful. We often see exhaustion as a status symbol, and believe productivity is synonymous with self-worth. In her younger years, my mother used to make comments to me about how I ran myself ragged, which is quite ironic, since I learned it from her. She would physically run herself into the ground, without demonstrating self-care and or stopping when tired. My mother would work herself to the point of exhaustion, never acknowledging her limitations until she was physically stopped in her tracks. I can say I haven't done this since my late 30s. I learned to give myself permission to say, "Enough. I'm tired and this can wait."

Even working for a company like Cisco where the culture exudes the message, "We live to work," I was able to maintain boundaries for myself. Most coworkers thought a 50- to 60-hour work week was a reflection of worthiness, a status symbol necessary to do their job well. I say it creates burnout and stifles creativity. Rarely did I work more than a 40-hour week. I am sure many would be shocked by my "lazy" work ethic. I didn't find it necessary to fill my role, nor did I see it helpful to work to the point of exhaustion. My philosophy was to "work to live"; my career didn't define me. It was what I did, not who I was. Don't get me wrong, I took pride in what I did and had integrity with my job, but it didn't own me. I learned a long time ago that once I am tired, very little productivity comes out of me anyway, so there was no point in pushing myself to exhaustion for sake of positioning myself as valuable.

Here's the deal—the most creative people rest and play regularly. According to Brian Sutton-Smith, "The opposite of play is not work; it is depression." It's so hard to play in a world where we attach our self-worth to what we produce.

Play and rest are critical to live with joy. It starts with letting go of exhaustion as some sort of status symbol and believing that being exhausted by working nonstop makes you valuable.

What is play?

Play is the time you spend without any specific purpose, with no need to get anywhere or get anything accomplished. It is something you don't want to stop doing. You lose track of time, you get in a zone and flow, and you stop being self-conscious. You lose yourself in play.

As adults, we often stop playing, because play is seen as irresponsible. It is, however, an act of great self-care and love. It is how we recharge, so that we can re-engage in being productive at our highest creative level. Play means totally checking out from anything other than being fully present to just play. You cannot be playing and updating your Facebook status, checking email, or checking sports scores on your mobile device. How often do adults really check out and play in life? Even when we say we are playing on a Saturday or Sunday, we rarely disconnect from the cyberworld and what's going on in it. I challenge you to have one day a week where you completely disconnect from all technology, disengage from responsibilities, and find time to play, to just be.

Playing as an adult is no different than how children play. They are all in, totally engaged in what they are doing with their whole hearts; it is pure being with no concern for anything but the moment they are participating in. I remember my son Trevor telling me about a time he was playing ball in the neighborhood with friends. His alarm went off on his watch to come home for dinner. He said he was having so much fun and didn't want to stop, and chose not to stop playing even though he knew there would be a consequence for being late. He was truly in the moment of play and at age nine, nothing could motivate him to stop.

My college friend Lisa and I have talked about this on several occasions as adults in our 40s. Why don't we laugh anymore like we did in college? We could literally be engaged in something of no importance and begin laughing until our bellies ached or someone peed their pants! This is play in the pure form, the bliss of being. We decided the reason we stopped playing is because we allowed ourselves to be sucked into being responsible adults and fun got de-prioritized. We committed to capturing as much fun as possible whenever we are together from now on!

Dance is play to me! I can lose myself by dancing the night away if there is great music playing and a dance floor. This was always the highlight of working a conference series in IT. I always had colleagues to hang out with and we would go out as a group and dance to the early hours. Being in open water—boating, swimming, paddle boarding—is also something that brings pure play out in me. Hiking in nature is a big-time play for me, too. One summer in Garmisch, Germany, I spent ten days with my fiancé, hiking all day long every day. It was bliss; no sense of time, no hurry, just communing with nature and him. The day would pass without me ever noticing what time it was, and I couldn't wait to get up the next day and do it all over again.

Contest can be a part of play, but competition is not. A contest is not about winning or dominating; it is about keeping the play going. Think about how animals play. They will purposely default themselves to extend the play. Watch two dogs play. They go back and forth between who is on top and who submits to the other, to keep the play going. Competition is about winning, being first, and proving yourself to be the best. It is not play.

For example, tennis is play for me. I love to play and keep the ball going. However, the minute it becomes a competition, play stops for me and I lose interest. The game is no longer extended play; it is all about starting and stopping to get ahead. When the ball stops, someone just "one-upped" the opponent. Golf is the same—I like to have fun and just play. Playing golf with serious competitive players takes all the fun out of the game for me.

Play cultivates creativity and fun. So, more play makes the world a more creative and, therefore, productive place. Everyone benefits. It is important that we model play to our children, friends, and coworkers. Better yet, let children model to you how to truly play.

The Path to Vulnerability: It's a Practice and a Lifestyle

Just as you don't stop exercising and eating healthy once you reach your optimal weight and health, you don't stop practicing vulnerability because you have been vulnerable. Here's how to keep it up.

Cultivate Creativity

Find something that allows your creative nature to flow. We are all creative; it is part of being human, but you have to tap into it. Unused creativity doesn't disappear. We often stop using our creativity because we were compared to others. If you were laughed at or a harsh comparison was made during art class as a child (which has happened to 80 percent of us, the shame or humiliation experienced may have prompted you to shut down your creative side. Studies show that around age ten, there is a drop in creativity in children. This may be due to put downs by teachers, other children, and not being able to express creativity without criticism.

My daughter, who is extremely artistically talented, has shut down this part of herself in the past due to her own self-criticism and comparing her work to others. She wants to do it perfectly out of the gate, instead of giving herself the space and freedom to explore. I recently saw a girlfriend do this to herself during an exercise at a workshop drawing mandalas. She was so focused on comparing her work and seeing it as inadequate to others, that she missed the point of the exercise and didn't allow herself to get lost in her own creativity.[10] Creativity is part of the human spirit and everyone has it. It doesn't mean everyone is meant to be a great artist or musician; it just means we are all meant to express our creativity, with no judgment or comparison.

Find White Space

Intuition comes from silence. Do you create white space in your life? You have to schedule it, just like everything else in your world. White space is the silence within where your intuition or spirit can talk to you. I'll discuss more about how to tap into this in chapter 8.

Let go of anxiety as a lifestyle. Calm is your greatest power. When you are calm and centered, you can tune into your native genius and have the ability to take action from your center, your core strength. Anxiety requires a numbing of some kind. It becomes easier to over-do, over-go, and over-achieve than feel. It's called over-functioning. Under-living is the same thing. Laziness isn't about exhaustion; it really means you are under-functioning and not sharing your gifts with the world.

Calm people breathe deeply and regularly and are comfortable in silence. If you can just breathe deeply for sixty seconds, you will probably dissolve 50 percent of any crazy feelings or anxiety. I notice how considerably calm I get the minute I bring my attention to my breath or take a yoga class with an emphasis on the breath.

Put Down the Shield

Cultivate authenticity by letting go of what people think. Realize that vulnerability leads to authenticity and it is a choice in every moment and every situation. Authenticity is the daily practice of letting go of who we think we should be, so we can let our true selves shine through. It is setting boundaries and allowing ourselves to be perfect in our imperfection. We invite grace, joy, and gratitude in our lives by the cultivation of authenticity through vulnerability.

I owe much of my own learning and experience of practicing vulnerability to Brené Brown and her research. If you'd like to learn more about vulnerability and how it can be your pathway to joy, I highly recommend her book *Daring Greatly*. Her TED Talks, available online, are also informative and enjoyable.

I think women in particular are ready to change our common definition of vulnerability and start showing up with their whole heart. One of the people I follow and admire, who is leading the way with vulnerability and whom I mentioned earlier, is Marianne Williamson. She is a spiritual teacher, thought leader, lecturer, and best-selling author, and most recently announced her candidacy for Congress. By using words like "love" freely,

Marianne demonstrates how her nonconformist approach to politics will be the birthplace for changing the game and healing our planet. She fiercely and courageously speaks her truth, like no one has done before in the political arena. I believe she is the spearhead that will create a wave of change and provide us all the courage to show up authentically. She is the standard all women leaders should start upholding—treating ourselves with honesty and self-worth so we can move through vulnerability to self-compassion, which is the topic of the next chapter.

Chapter 6

Self-Compassion:
Being Your Own Best Friend

*"Happiness is when what you think, what you say, and what you do
are in harmony. Always aim at complete harmony of thought and
word and deed. Always aim at purifying your thoughts and everything
will be well."*

—Mahatma Gandhi

*O*ne of the best ways to improve your social skills is to behave in a congruent manner and communicate in an authentic way. People truly respect and appreciate authentic communication. Others experience an ease and enjoyment when your thoughts, words, and actions are aligned. Plus, it leaves you feeling powerful and good about yourself. When your thoughts, words, and actions are in alignment, it comes through in clear communication and a powerful presence.

Once you think of your relationship with yourself as primary, your relationship with others—and the world—becomes a reflection of your inner self. When we invest more energy in developing our spiritual lives, the outer world begins to take care of itself. Self-compassion is a foundational ingredient needed to align yourself in harmony.

There is often a misconception about self-compassion in our culture, a belief that it is synonymous with self-indulgence, conceit, and ego. Self-compassion is actually being your own best friend. It is offering yourself love, kindness, support, and encouragement. Being self-compassionate is a great motivator to create and achieve what you want in life. You are, after all, the one constant in your life from birth to death, so you should learn to treat yourself with the same compassion you would provide a dear friend or loved one. Being there for yourself emotionally and truly counting on yourself is one of the most critical components to inner harmony and happiness. We crave compassion from others, yet that needs to be fulfilled within ourselves first. Then, we are no longer dependent on something external and others will begin reflecting compassion back to you.

Here is an example. Prior to discovering how to be emotionally available and supportive to myself, I would attract and select similar men, ones who were emotionally absent and not truly capable of providing compassion. It was a direct correlation: the degree I was emotionally available to myself was the degree men in my life were emotionally available to me. I was looking for them to give me what I ultimately needed to learn to give myself. I have found that whenever I am upset because someone is not giving me what I want or need emotionally, it is a tell-tale sign that I need to be offering myself exactly that. It's the perfect cue that I need to go within and practice some self-care.

Now that I am more self-aware and compassionate to myself on a regular basis, not only is my life more harmonious, I am no longer attracted to emotionally unavailable men. In fact, over the last couple of years, I have attracted some beautiful men with open hearts and the ability to be empathic and compassionate. Self-compassion is about being there for yourself in a steadfast way.

Why Aren't We Taught Self-Compassion?

Many earlier generations believed that the best motivator for children to achieve and accomplish things in life was to berate, punish, and even provoke shame when they didn't meet expectations, made a mistake, or failed. But this behavior and verbal lashing has the opposite effect on our motivation level and can also create mistrust. If you knew you would get a lashing from your parent and would be met with little to no understanding or compassion, you would be encouraged to lie to protect yourself.

I remember as a young teenager I had a swim teammate whose father was a well-known swim coach. He put so much pressure on her to perform that she would lie to him about her event times when he wasn't at a meet. She was a great swimmer, yet her motivation and love for the sport was dwindling from the pressure to be perfect and the berating she experienced when she didn't meet his expectations.

My own brother also suffered from the same type of parenting. Because he was the oldest and the only boy, my parents were particularly hard on him. When my mom was raising my brother, who was fourteen years older than I was, my mother's parenting was still completely steeped in what her parents had demonstrated for her. My brother learned to be dishonest at a very young age to avoid the shame and lashing he knew he had in store. Unfortunately, he never healed his shame and therefore never learned to live honestly, especially with himself. He died at age sixty-two, severely obese and having never realized any true happiness or fulfillment in life. He had always been desperately in search of love and compassion, as he had never learned to provide it to himself.

From my own experience as a child, I knew mistakes were considered unacceptable and some form of punishment usually followed, all under the guise of teaching me to be responsible. One Sunday evening, after spending an entire weekend at an AAU swim meet in downtown St. Louis, one of my teammate's parents brought me home. I was about fourteen. It was very late, I was exhausted, and it was a cold winter night. I had a giant duffle bag full of swim gear and towels, but I could not find my house key. My mother and stepfather were out for the evening. This was way before cell phones, so I had to go to a neighbor's house and call my older sister who was in her twenties at the time and lived about thirty minutes away. She drove over to let me in with her key, and of course, let our mother know how she had been inconvenienced by my irresponsibility. Once I got inside and dumped my bag out on the floor, there was the key! Even though I hadn't been "irresponsible" by forgetting it, I was still grounded for two weeks. The truth is, though, that this really didn't teach me to be responsible—it just made me frustrated because I was doing my best and had still made an error. The natural consequence of not getting in the house, having to go to a neighbor's, and waiting for my sister was lesson enough to put the house key somewhere easy to find in the future.

Imagine this same situation being handled with compassion instead with the attitude that I screwed up. It would sound something like this: "Lisa, it must have really been a bummer coming home alone late at night, exhausted, just wanting to get in to the warm house. I know you dreaded calling your sister, because she probably wasn't happy about driving out here to let you in. What do you think you could do differently in the future to ensure that your key is with you or easily found when needed? Is there anything I can do to support you?"

The bottom line is that no type of berating, blaming, or shame helps anyone do better. It actually discourages attempts to put yourself out there and do your best. Learning to give yourself compassion is exactly what you need to achieve and create a successful, harmonious life. It is a vital ingredient that is often overlooked in spiritual growth and happiness.

Self-Esteem and Self-Compassion Are Not the Same Thing

Self-esteem has been a buzzword in our society for the last few decades, especially in regards to raising children. Unfortunately, we are beginning to create a world of approval addicts and narcissists who only believe they are okay if others approve of them and perceive them to be successful, beautiful, or important. It is the "every kid gets a trophy" syndrome. You can see it in the ridiculous god-like regard we give people who have achieved athletic and financial success. They are, after all, just people making mistakes. They are even more at risk of living from their ego instead of their true spiritual nature, because they are revered by the public. They live from win to win, feeling superior and lacking any self-understanding and deep connection because of the shining substitute of praise. Lance Armstrong is a perfect example. In a recent interview with Oprah, it became so clear to me that he was just a man, arrogant and obsessed with winning to the point that he had lost his integrity and moral compass. He actually said, "I didn't even think there was anything wrong with doping and lying about it at the time." He was consumed with winning at any cost and it cost him his integrity and understanding of what is really important in life.

This type of external validation and desire to win becomes a never-ending quest for recognition through achievements, being liked, job status, money, and many other things. The problem is that it only allows for a short, temporary "feel-good," always needing more. It leaves us dependent on external factors we have no control over, and when we don't get it, our feeling of worthiness and belonging is at stake. Filling the fuel tank of our soul happens from the self-validation, empathy, and compassion we give ourselves—not through self-esteem, which is external and dependent on others.

As I let go of who I was in the corporate world (which included status, income, job security, and company culture), I began to learn how critical it is to be my own biggest fan, supporter, and believer. I was leaving one identity behind and stepping into a new me, a middle ground of "no longer, but not yet." I have realized that, without compassion and self-encouragement, there is no way for me to navigate this death-to-rebirth transition successfully. Believing in myself is the true motivation moving me forward toward my goals and dreams. It is necessary for anyone who wants to make their dreams come true, along with accepting that it is okay to fail and knowing you will learn lessons from the willingness to be courageous and take a chance on your passion. At times I feel like I have jumped off a cliff, but I trust the process by demonstrating self-compassion. I trust that I will either grow wings to soar or instead find a soft place to land.

I once heard an inspiring interview with Jeff Bezos, founder of Amazon.com. He had a successful Wall Street career when his passion for the internet and reading sparked him to start the online book store. He started the business in his garage with his wife. As he contemplated his plans and fear came up, he knew that he wouldn't regret failing—he would only regret not trying. He uses what he terms "Regret Minimization Framework." When contemplating a decision, he imagines he is eighty years old looking back at his life. He asks himself if he would regret making the decision to not try something. If the answer is "yes," he moves forward with excitement, knowing it is the right decision even if he fails. This is a beautiful example of self-compassion that can motivate and encourage us to act on our own passion and creativity.

Self-Kindness

The best way to begin practicing self-compassion is by learning to speak to yourself with kindness. Supportive and tender self-talk is critical when life's circumstances become difficult or overwhelming and you feel panic, fear, or anxiety—this is how we find harmony within. Speak to yourself exactly the same way you would speak to someone you deeply care about. Think of the way you speak to a child, a close friend, or a family member, and then offer that same dialogue to yourself when you are struggling with life or are just in a tough situation. It sounds something like this: "I know this is hard and I am sorry it doesn't feel good, but you are so capable of doing this. I know you will get through this. I believe in you and love you no matter what—win or lose." Or ask yourself: "What would be the most supportive and loving thing I could do for myself right now?" This dialogue is a moment-to-moment choice that requires becoming acutely aware and conscious of your thoughts. It is living life fully present instead of going through the motions on autopilot.

The good news is most women already know how to offer this type of compassion and support to one another, as we tend to be natural nurturers.

The bad news is most of us are in the habit of talking to ourselves in a way we wouldn't even talk to someone we disliked! Many of us have been talking negatively to ourselves for so long that it has become habit—we are not consciously aware of our negative internal dialogue. We berate ourselves and call ourselves names, sometimes silently and sometimes out loud. It usually goes something like this: "you idiot," "well that was stupid," "pull it together," "you will never be good at this," "I can't do it," and the list goes on. There is a tendency to be more concerned with how others perceive us, instead of tuning in to our own needs.

We have all noticed a stressed mother (or have been that mother) on a plane who has a small child or infant crying or having a tantrum during the flight. This situation can create anxiety for almost anyone. The child is uncomfortable and we want to soothe them. There are two options:

We attempt to soothe the child, feeling stressed and possibly concerned or embarrassed about what other people are thinking because we may be disturbing them. Our anxiety will then transfer to the child and just add more agitation to the situation. It will keep us from being truly connected and compassionate. Or...

What if we actually begin to soothe ourselves with compassionate self-talk? We could say to ourselves, "This is tough but it is okay, it will pass. Just stay calm; breathe and stay present." The more calm and compassionate we are to ourselves, the more calm and compassionate we can be to the child, whether or not we are able to soothe them. I remember when my daughter was a newborn and would have endless crying spells. I felt like a failure because I couldn't soothe her, and I became more stressed and upset the longer she cried. The minute my mom would take her from me with a calm compassionate energy, my baby girl would relax and stop crying.

Think about how often you hear someone (or even hear yourself) say something like, "That was stupid," after making a minor mistake. This is the perfect opportunity to create awareness and begin practicing loving self-compassion. Whenever I hear someone put themselves down, I usually say something like, "I care too much about you to hear you talk to yourself that way. Please treat yourself with more love and compassion."

You need to give yourself exactly the same encouragement and support you would give to your daughter, sister, and best friend. It will allow you to create self-love and a strong sense of self-worth so you can persevere, create, and find peace. Because you are already great at encouraging and supporting others, you have the skill set—you only need to turn it inward and support yourself in being the very best you.

Becoming mindful of your self-talk is the key. Notice what you are saying to yourself. Is it compassionate, forgiving, accepting, and kind? If not, shift it. It takes practice.

So many women sacrifice their own needs by focusing their attention on the constant care and encouragement of others. This can only continue for so long before we become completely depleted. It fosters one-sided, codependent relationships. I know this, because I *was* one of those codependent people. By loving ourselves and being kind and compassionate within, we will be that much more available to truly comfort one another. It takes us right back to those airplane safety directions I mentioned earlier. *Place the oxygen mask on yourself first before assisting children or others.* Someone once told me that she always thought those directions were odd and they didn't make sense to her. She wanted to know, "Why wouldn't I help my children first?" The reason is that the degree to which you respect, honor, care, love, and have compassion for yourself is directly proportionate to the degree you can give to others. How long can you help your child, if you cannot breathe in life? Put the oxygen mask on yourself first, so you have something to truly share with others.

We Are All in the Same Boat

The simple realization that other people experience the same feelings, doubts, and difficulties in life as you do brings a feeling of acceptance and comfort to a difficult situation. It is common to feel isolated, as if we are the only one experiencing struggle, fear, uncertainty, or failure. I promise, no emotion or negative life circumstance is unique to any one individual. If it is happening to you, it has and will happen to others. Remind yourself that you are not alone, that we all share a common humanity, and that should be enough to bring you into a self-compassionate state of mind. I remind myself regularly that even though others can appear as perfect or having it all together on the surface, it is not true. Everyone struggles with not feeling good enough. We are all human and we are all wounded at some level, no matter what the outward behavior. No one is better than anyone else and the minute you put someone above you, you have lowered your sense of worth. Don't do it. We are all human, doing the best we can with the tools we have, perfect in our imperfection.

I remember doing a high ropes course at the Miraval Resort in Arizona. High ropes courses are an agility challenge, usually involving heights and general physical challenges. The challenge was to climb a telephone pole to the top, stand on a 2x1-foot platform, then jump off. I made it to the top, but could not figure out how to hike my leg up and over the platform to achieve a standing position. I was panicked, asking for advice from the instructors and saying out loud, "I can't do it." I asked to jump from there; they said no. I was in tears and felt completely incapable. Suddenly, with no choices left, I somehow found within me a little voice of encouragement through common humanity. I told myself there had been many people before me that had accomplished this physical feat and many of them were probably not half as athletic as me. If others had felt the fear and still done it, then I could do it too. That is all it took—magically I was on top of the platform.

I believe this is one of the reasons that group counseling and peer learning is so effective. People feel down and overwhelmed with life—and then they realize that others struggle with the exact same thing or something similar. Self-compassion is sparked though the comfort in knowing there is a common humanity among us and we are not alone in our experience. Knowing we are no different than any other human being and reaching out of that isolation while struggling brings hope and peace.

So anytime you feel the world is crashing down on you, reach for the comfort of knowing there are many people in the world who have felt exactly what you are experiencing, or who may be feeling that way right now. As a member of the human race, you are never alone.

Mindfulness

Becoming self-compassionate requires that you manage your mind. When we learn to direct our thoughts and words toward the outcome we desire, we ignite grace.

Self-compassion is something we give ourselves, that reassures us that we are okay, we are good enough, we are worthy of love and kindness. And the first step is to become aware of the self-talk, so you can cancel negative thoughts and replace them with loving, understanding, and kindness. This is where mindfulness comes in. It is necessary in order to provide compassion, love, kindness, encouragement, and overall understanding to ourselves.

I was well into my thirties before I learned I had the power to choose my thoughts. Prior to that, my random thoughts dictated my decisions, desperately seeking love and belonging. I was unconscious to what I was thinking, just mindlessly susceptible to wherever my thoughts took me. Thoughts create your feelings, and then feelings create your emotions. (Remember, emotions are your feelings expressed outwardly.) So, our thoughts create our experiences—not our external circumstances, but how we choose to perceive those circumstances. What we choose to think can become our reality. My mother used to say, "You can't control your feelings, they just are." So not true! When I choose my thoughts and beliefs, I have control over my feelings.

Being mindful means becoming fully present to the moment, becoming completely tuned in to what you are experiencing, and then observing your experience. It is an attunement to the divine presence within and around you. It is the realization that you are not a victim of circumstance or other people's intentions. By staying focused on your *own* intentions, you can choose to always give back to life in every given moment. Mindfulness is the vigilant practice of constantly bringing yourself back to the present moment and noticing or observing what you are thinking or telling yourself.

You can only live in and control one moment at a time. This moment, right now, is where your power lies—not the past or the future. "Mind-made" suffering dissolves when you are present. The other advantages of mindfulness are clarity, calmness, and positivity.

When you are in the moment, you have greater focus, and things flow naturally to you and through you with clarity. This is extremely advantageous for conversations, when working, while creating, or while playing a sport. Calmness permeates your being when you feel centered, relaxed, and at ease in all that you do. Fear diminishes if there is no projection into the future or reflection on past experiences. When calm takes over, fear falls away—and so do negative emotions and thoughts. You move into a positive state.

To learn more about self-compassion, check out Dr. Kristin Neff's TED Talk, and take her online test at www.self-compassion.org to find out how self-compassionate you are. Share it with your partner or anyone you are considering dating. The more self-compassionate we are, the more compassionate we are with others. Practicing self-compassion is critical and one of the best-kept secrets when it comes to living our potential and finding harmony within— and when we can live in that harmony, we are able to recognize and live in accordance to our inner wisdom, as we will learn in the next chapter.

Chapter 7

Your Inner Wisdom: Knowing from Within

"There is no need to soar heavenward while dragging the body behind as a burden...Use the body itself as a means of transcendence."

—Kathlyn Hendricks

It appears the majority of Western culture walks around completely in the left hemisphere of the brain, totally unaware that there is even a body attached to their head. This is what I call living life from our head. Our body has so much more wisdom and knows so much more than just our head. Our bodies are amazing compasses that speak to us constantly, but we must be tuned into that wisdom. In other words, we must be fully embodied. So often we live from our "shoulds" or personal religions, which are directed by thoughts and beliefs, yet the body is telling us to do something different that is truly for our best and highest good. If we are not embodied and are only living in our head, there is no way to hear this inner wisdom.

My business success in the technology industry was driven by my ability to connect with others and form trusting relationships. As many of us have heard, people do business with people they like, feel connected to, and trust. It seems that as technology continues to advance and keep us better connected as human beings, disconnection is growing between people. The ability to be truly empathetic and connect to others from the heart is rapidly diminishing. We are all human beings and need to feel connected, yet that fact is so discounted and overlooked. Connectedness is critical for true success in any type of relationship, including business. For me, the lack of it made a work life full of shallow relationships that ultimately left me feeling dissatisfied and as if there was no meaningful purpose—it was often just a very busy and distracted lifestyle of attempting to look good or know more in front of colleagues.

Thought, and the Left and Right Brain

The brain is composed of right and left hemispheres, each of which is responsible for different behaviors. The left hemisphere controls language, hearing, and handwriting. The left brain is logical and analytical. The right hemisphere controls the other sensory activities and allows for creativity and visualization. The right brain specializes in visual face recognition, spatial aptitude, music, and insight. The left brain controls the right side of the body and the right brain controls the left side of the body. While each hemisphere is necessary for a human to have a complete experience of the world around him, some people tend to use one hemisphere of their brain more than the other hemisphere. If you want to find out if you are right or left brain dominant, you can find many free tests you can take online with a simple keyword search.

This left hemisphere of our brain is basically a giant database or hard drive, a collection of all the things we've learned: language, how to operate something, how to work on cars, sewing, driving, eating, walking—everything. Logical mental processes are only one aspect of our intelligence, yet most believe this is where all of our intelligence lies. Therefore, they rely solely on the left hemisphere for everything they do and decide in life. But the left brain is not how we connect to the present moment and it is not how we tap into our inner wisdom and intuition. We cannot form meaningful relationships with others through intellect alone. The vastness of being is so much greater than the left brain of pure "thinking."

Of course, we need the left brain to get us where we need to be on time and to perform all types of tasks, from speaking to mathematics. But some of the most recognized scientific investigators and inventors would tell you they often formed their hypothesis from a hunch. The left brain actually works at its highest potential when we use it to carry out action or to create what we want in our lives.

I love the phrase, "The mind is a great servant, but a terrible master." We have been taught to make the mind our master. Our thoughts often control us and dictate what we do in the world—we believe in them and invest in them as if they were gospel. We have allowed the thinking mind to serve as our master to the point that we have no way of knowing whether what we are thinking is best for us. We have learned to approach the world and our relationships, with others and with ourselves, through this uncontrolled thinking rather than from our hearts and whole being. The left brain does not foster presence, creativity, love, or peace; these reside in the right hemisphere of the brain. The right brain is also the home of your connection to spirit, higher consciousness, and the ability to see everything as energy. After all, if you break it down, everything is just energy vibrating at various frequencies and constantly changing at various rates, right?

Left-brain thinking is what allowed me to excel in many ways in the business world. I could usually rely on my thinking and analytical mind to figure out solutions or next steps to accomplish most tasks or projects. In fact, this became such a default mode of operation that I thought it was the only way to solve a problem, get over an obstacle, or find a solution. When I couldn't think of an answer, though, I became immobilized and stuck. I felt inferior among all the brilliant and highly educated minds around me. At times, fear and panic would set in, which immobilized me even more. I would feel defeated and would usually withdraw and shut down.

I finally understood the extent of this problem after a romantic breakup. I believed I could find my way to resolution or process grief from thinking and analyzing my way out of the pain. This actually inhibited my progress and stuck me in a cycle of pain—what I call mental masturbation. Fortunately, I have always been an athlete and stayed in good physical shape, which became my ally for emotional survival. Notice I said survival, not healing. I would be so panicked with fear at times, my mind would race and I would actually pace frantically. I would force myself to put on my running shoes and then run as long and as hard as I could. Then a shift would happen. I was present in my body at last. Adrenaline would subside and I would feel calm again. I had found my zone. The suffering would temporarily dissolve. But the cycle would always continue, as my thoughts and beliefs went uninvestigated or unaddressed and begin all over.

The point is, some things in life cannot be processed by thought. They have to be processed through the heart and bodily sensation. Getting out of your head allows emotional processing. Grief is a perfect example. Grief has to be felt, stages experienced with no time limits, before processing enough to get to the other side—which leads to more strength and greater wisdom. There are no shortcuts; there is no thinking your way out of the loss and adjusting to the life's changes with just the mind. Any attempts to avoid or mask grief only slow the process and forces the pain to come out in a very unhealthy way. Yet, we don't seem to honor emotional healing in our society as a whole. We encourage people to take antidepressants and to just put our emotions away and get over them as quickly as possible. Like the saying, "The quickest way to get over someone is to get on top of someone else." Could that be any unhealthier or more disrespectful to both you and the person you are using? Of course, because these kinds of shortcuts are not built on any kind of foundation, they are certain to collapse—and you will find yourself at ground zero again.

Being Present

Try this exercise to determine if you are fully embodied right now, or just living in the left brain. You can also use this at any time to become present and embodied throughout your day. This is how you get into your body and in touch with your feelings. The body never lies and embodies great wisdom. In fact, your heart actually sends more messages to your body than your brain sends.

1. Without moving, close your eyes.
2. Begin a *very slow* scan of your body—take no less than a full minute to do this. Start at your head and work through your neck and throat, chest, shoulders, arms, fingertips, back, abdominal region, buttocks, quadriceps, hamstrings, knees, calves, shins, and finally your feet and toes. Allow yourself to fully sense and become aware of every sensation in your physical body.
3. As you perform this scan, notice where you feel any discomfort, tension, aches, or pressure.
4. Pause at these identified areas of stress and rearrange your body (if needed) to a more comfortable position.
5. Take three long, complete breaths, breathing from the stressed area of your body. Visualize drinking oxygen into that particular area.
6. Repeat this process for each area of tension within your body, until you feel completely relaxed, joyful, and at peace.

I bet you weren't even aware before starting this body scan—especially if you were sitting at your computer—that you were in some awkward position causing stress in your body. Now that you are embodied and not just in your left brain, do you feel more relaxed, fluid, and receptive? If not, repeat the steps again. This is a great practice to do any time of day. It is a way to pause, take a break, and get centered, which will allow you to be more effective with whatever you are doing.

As we discussed in the chapter on self-compassion, self-love is the first and most important step in becoming capable of experiencing a feeling of joy, peace, and love from within. However, people who are right brain dominant or balanced between both hemispheres often find it easier to naturally tap into this part of their being, as opposed to left brain dominant people. The good news is that you can achieve balance with practice; it is like any other muscle training. It requires diligent attention to your moods, and when you are not joyful or calm, immediately question what you are thinking—then become present by doing the exercise to get out of your head and fully into your body again. Jill, the spiritual therapist I mentioned earlier, taught me that the sign of mastery isn't that we never fall off, but how quickly we can jump back in to joy. There was a point in my life where it would take me weeks or days to jump back into joy; now it happens rarely and only for a few hours at most.

When I feel any level of unease, anxiety, or stress, that is my cue to get quiet, hit the pause button, and go inside myself to determine the source of my suffering. Breathing and scanning my physical body immediately brings me out of my thoughts and into the present moment. Breath is a powerful tool, yet many people are completely unaware of their breathing. Most don't ever use their lungs to capacity by fully inhaling and exhaling, and stale air sits in the bottom. When people become stressed or fearful, the breath restricts even more, which causes even more tension. But breathing is the cure! When we get out of our heads and properly breathe, we make wiser decisions. This is also where you can sense the connection to the universe, God, the higher conscious, whatever you believe makes us all one. I will refer to this as the mind-body-spirit connection.

The mind-body-spirit connection is represented by a triangle. These are the three aspects that encompass our wholeness as a being. To be fully embodied and truly whole, all three need to be actively communicating, connected, and balanced. Just as a triangle cannot be balanced without all three sides aligned and connected, our whole being is balanced when our three aspects are aligned. Our intuition, our inner wisdom, our all-knowing self, only emerges when we truly become balanced in mind, body, and spirit.

My mother told me at a very young age that the more I listen and act based on the little quiet voice within, the stronger and louder the voice becomes.

Some people call this "gut instinct," or intuition, and most will tell you it is usually right on, though many don't choose to follow it. Here is an example that everyone has experienced: Remember a time when you did something or made a choice that created an unwanted result, and afterwards you said to yourself, "Dang it, something told me not to do that!" Practice listening to your inner voice. Follow the guidance, and that voice will become louder and more obvious. The way to really hear that voice loud and clear is to get out of the thinking mind, get still, and be fully present in your body. We all have the ability to be completely connected with our intuition or all-knowing self. Intuition is not pie in the sky or some hocus pocus; it is simply greatness beyond the thinking mind.

Malcolm Gladwell's book *Blink: The Power of Thinking without Thinking* documents many examples of our inner knowing or intuition working independently of the thinking mind, or left brain. This is very similar to how we can't process heartbreak with the thinking mind, or how a great musician or artist doesn't create from the left brain; it just flows to them from something greater than thought. There is simply an acceptance, a presence, or a knowing that logic can't understand.

For example, Gladwell told of a sixth century BC marble statue that was being sold to a California museum for $10 million. Geologists and curators carefully studied the piece to make sure it was truly authentic. They found it was, and relayed the results to the museum. Afterwards, two other museum directors took one quick look at the statue and immediately received energetic impressions saying "fresh" and "intuitive repulsion." The museum directors weren't studying the statue for aspects of authenticity as the scientists did. It was simply an immediate knowing that the statue was fake; in contrast to the thinking mind that analyzed the statue at great length and couldn't detect the falsehood. The statue was in turn proven to be fraudulent with further research. This story demonstrates how when one is truly in the present moment, sensing everything as energy from the right brain, universal intelligence or inner wisdom comes straight through. However, the truth remains that the thinking mind is not what ultimately discovered the fraud. The statue's creators developed the fake with the goal of tricking the scientific thinking mind. But there is no way to trick our inner knowing. We all have the ability to tap into this by being fully present and connected to the mind, body, and spirit.

I personally experienced this when my fiancé Greg was shipped to Iraq for a year. He was an Army Blackhawk helicopter pilot and the first few months he was there, those birds were being shot out of the sky daily. Greg's mother, sisters, and daughters were worried to death about his safety. They were buying into fear delivered from the media. But I had this all-knowing feeling that he was meant to come home just fine, and I truly never worried or stressed about his safety. I felt it in my core as truth. He came home twelve months later, and he was physically unharmed.

I used to be startled easily if someone entered a room while my back was turned and simply said "Lisa." I would scream and jump out of my skin. My kids and boyfriends would get quite a kick out of walking up behind me in the laundry room and saying my name to watch my reaction. I use to think this just meant I was sensitive. But the truth was, I was deep in thought, not present in my surroundings or in my body. Therefore, I was abruptly startled back to the present by hearing an unexpected sound from another human. Talk about not being in my body! The same thing happens when the wind abruptly slams a door slams. Our startled response is due to our inability to process the noise. We are not fully aware; only the eyes are available to send a signal to the brain. When we are fully embodied and present, we are operating at our highest frequency, fine-tuned to access and receive anything we need from the universe or God or whatever we call our higher Source, as well as our inner wisdom.

So then why are we so prone to neglect the physical body and live in our heads? For many people, it is because we learn to disconnect from the body when we experience trauma of any kind, as a defense mechanism. We can do this very easily by staying distracted and making ourselves busy. We abandon the body to avoid the uncomfortable feelings that arise within. But these uncomfortable feelings and inner callings from our soul beg to be processed and released, so our spirits may soar and we can get back to being whole and pure. The soul is your eternal essence, your connection to God; your spirit is your expression of that essence in the physical world. Eastern cultures and

Native American traditions teach children meditation at a very young age, which keep them grounded and connected to the present. Western society, on the other hand, seems to have made intellect king—though I am beginning to see the pendulum swing in the other direction. Western culture is opening to more spiritual practices as a way of life. This is really good news, and something I get really excited about.

Yoga: Becoming Embodied with the Breath

One of those spiritual practices is yoga. Connecting to the breath is the quickest and easiest way to become present in your body, which is why yoga is such an amazing mind-body-spirit tool. Yoga began as a science and has been practiced for more than 3,000 years. It consists of ancient theories, observations, and principles about the mind-body-spirit connection that Western medicine is now studying and, in some cases, proving. According to research, heart surgery patients can drastically speed up recovery through yoga, and it has provided relief for many soldiers suffering from post-traumatic stress syndrome (PTSS), when therapy and pharmaceuticals have failed.[11]

There are more than one hundred different schools of yoga. Hatha and Vinyasa Flow yoga are the most popular and common in America. Physically, yoga includes movements, postures, and breathing techniques. The whole system is built on three main structures: the postures/poses (or Asanas), the breathing (or Pranayama), and meditation. To receive yoga's maximum benefits, all three structures require practice. The word yoga means "to join or yoke together." Sanskrit is an ancient dead language, but is still used in yoga today. One of the most commonly known poses is "down dog" or "downward facing dog." The Sanskrit word for this is "Ado Muka Shvansasana." "Prana" is the Sanskrit word for breath; it means "life force."

In daily life, we often tell someone to take a deep breath when they become panicked, although we don't really know the source of this common wisdom. It works because taking a deep breath sends oxygen to our lungs, then to our cardiopulmonary system, which gets oxygen to our entire body. The actual act of a big inhale immediately relaxes our muscles. This sends our body a signal to relax, which then diminishes the fight or flight response. Anytime you need to diminish suffering, anxieties, and poor decisions, take a deep breath. It only takes ninety seconds for an emotion to pass if we don't take action on it. A simple breath will instantly return us to the present moment. Pranayama, the regular practice of yogic breathing exercise, teaches us to activate breath in all of life's circumstances.

Yoga is also a good way to start understanding your reactions in life. What your body learns on the mat translates metaphorically to things you can apply to your everyday life. I have learned to breathe through a difficult or uncomfortable yoga pose by focusing on the contracting and expanding of my body. I no longer panic or focus on wanting to get out of that pose, but realize it is just a sensation and an experience. That way, it becomes more of an observation. Then, as I focus on the fluidity of my breath, I begin to move like water. We are 80 percent water and even when water is moving or flowing, there is also stillness. For me, yoga is meditation in motion.

Mindful Meditation

Mindful meditation means to be settled, still, and clear of worry. In the past decade, meditation has become more mainstream and is now practiced by athletes, business professionals, students, and even inmates. Finding peace of mind through mediation teaches us to respond to life instead of unconsciously reacting to life. The simplest form is to sit comfortably and quietly, bringing your attention to your breath and your heart center. When you catch your thoughts drifting, gently remind yourself without judgment to bring your attention back to the breath.

What I have learned about myself, and suspect is true for many, is that I tend to dissociate from certain feelings and emotions when a life event triggers a traumatic subconscious memory. For me it is usually the feelings of abandonment or feelings of "I'm not as good as other people" that I experienced and learned as a young child. I learned to dissociate from those feelings as a way of surviving something that was too scary for me to emotionally process at the time. However, refusing to feel it simply suppressed it in my subconscious; it didn't make it disappear. As an adult, my subconscious began revealing this long-suppressed trauma and fear to my conscious mind—usually by drawing people and situations to myself to specifically bring this stuff up. Through the practice of meditation, we can bring these wounds to the surface to be experienced and released, so that we may ultimately heal and upgrade ourselves to wholeness. This process releases us as prisoners of our past so our lives can be full of joy and love.

When I allowed these emotions to arise and didn't try to analyze them away with my thinking mind, I became a witness to the experience, and the emotions would pass pretty quickly. This became my practice—the observation and witnessing of my thoughts whenever I felt uncomfortable emotionally. Over time, the emotions were triggered less often and the impact or severity became less and less. In allowing ourselves to observe these uncomfortable sensations, they are a path home to our divine truth. We will continue to subconsciously call up or create experiences to trigger these feelings until we fully heal and release them. This is our soul giving us directions to the path that will bring us home to wholeness. You can either avoid the emotions at all costs, or go through them mindfully to heal once and for all.

Here is how to use meditation to become a witness to your thoughts and emotions. It is basically taking a detached perspective of yourself:

1. Sit quietly, settle in, and become still by focusing on your breathing. For me, it helps to call in divine light for support and protection, but you may want to call in God, your angels, or whatever resonates with you.
2. As you look in front of you, select something to focus on. Soften your gaze, with your eyes still on that one object, and broaden your perspective without focusing on anything. Your gaze is on the one object, but you are not really seeing or analyzing it.
3. Notice everything around or outside of the object, but keep your eyes trained on the object in the center.
4. Keep practicing steps 1 and 2 until you feel a shift or find yourself in a peaceful zone.
5. Now, go to the place behind your eyes. Ask yourself: Who is doing the seeing? Who sees? (If your reaction to this question was, "Well, who

else would be seeing but *me?*" ask yourself, "Who is the *me?* Who is asking, 'Who am I?'")

Write down what thoughts came up for you and any accompanying feelings.

_____

_____

_____

Repeat the process of becoming still. This time, you will observe your thoughts. Tune in to whatever you are thinking about right now, really become aware of it. Think about it like the thinker is a separate entity, because it is—it is your ego, not your soul or spirit. Experience these sensations or emotions with detached observation.

Now ask: Who is doing the thinking? Who is the thinker?

Write down what you noticed. Did you become peaceful? Calmer? Curious? Any sensations?

_____

_____

_____

I usually feel calmness and an immediate release from any anxiety; I hope that your experience was similar. As soon as you allow yourself to experience the sensations in your body, adopting a perspective of compassion and non-judgment is necessary for releasing and moving though the experience. By not labeling anything as right or wrong, you remove the ego and don't allow the experience to have any power over you. I encourage you to make this a regular practice. Find a certain time every day that you can dedicate just one or two minutes to it. Soon you will begin tapping into your true nature of peacefulness and calm. This is a great practice to use when struggling with a choice or decision in life, because you will be able to tap into your greatest wisdom and find the best answer. Your greatest answers in life lie within.

When we continue to resist and suppress feelings of discomfort, they will persist, and without acknowledging and processing them, the unattended feelings, emotions, and wounds will eventually manifest themselves in the physical body. I believe most diseases are manifestations of emotional dis-ease or imbalances within our mind-body-spirit. We are one elaborate system; our bodies are not separate from our spiritual and mental being. Louise Hay does a great job of explaining this in her book, *You Can Heal Your Life*. I highly recommend it to help understand the correlation between our thoughts and emotions, and how they can physically manifest in our bodies and health.

Your inner wisdom is accessed when you are fully embodied and present. Living from the thinking mind will never allow you to create an authentic life you love. There are so many resources available today to support you on this journey. If you are ready, those resources and guideposts just will reveal themselves with perfect timing. Take the journey; it is so rewarding to realize you are not your past and to return to the knowing that you always were and always will be a perfect expression of love.

"The most rigid structures, the most impervious to change, will collapse first. Moving through change and uncomfortable situations with grace, trust, and ease allows us to transform, evolve, and transcend the chaos of thought, or the monkey mind."

—**Eckhart Tolle**

Chapter 8

Living Life Outward

"Many of life's failures are people who did not realize how close they were to success when they gave up."

—Thomas Edison

*I*f your life's purpose is to live a life of adventure, to create joy, to make a difference, or to go beyond, then you must allow yourself to dream and take action on those dreams. Living life in purely realistic terms will cost you a life devoid of deep satisfaction and fulfillment.

Explore and find your dreams. Give yourself permission to not just dream, but to dream big.

Tony Hsieh, the CEO of Zappos.com, has a principle of always setting the goal or dream beyond what you think you can accomplish. Most of us do the opposite. We don't allow ourselves to think and dream big, and therein lies the limitations for what we experience. Living in the limitations of what is realistic based on the now stifles the ability to create and achieve new and amazing outcomes. I believe what makes Tony Hsieh one of the best entrepreneurs in the world is that everything he does is built on a foundation of exceptional customer service, community creation, and alignment with contributing to the greater good of humanity. That is just great karma! When dreams are not just ego-based, but eco-based, then you know your passion and purpose are aligned with the Universe. With the right action, success is inevitable.

Step 1: Allow yourself to dream. Open to infinite possibilities.
All new possibilities emerge when we open ourselves to dreaming, when we allow our imagination to create. What if there were no limits? What would you be willing to try, create, or imagine? Think about all the inventions in the world, the amazing physical feats people have accomplished or overcome, the wonderful books that have been written. Most great gifts to the world started with someone dreaming up the possibility. Give yourself permission to dream, and let go of the logical mind. The logical mind is risk averse and always operating from past experience. You cannot dream and create new possibilities from the logical mind. So let go, dream big.

Step 2: Be willing to take action, to become more committed to your dream than your fear and doubt.
Success happens by taking action, any action; even tiny steps move you closer to your goal. I once heard someone say they wished they had found their calling, a career they were passionate about, but now it's too late because they are almost fifty years old. I say: You are going to turn fifty no matter what, so why *not* be fifty or sixty when you find your purpose and passion?

What does age have to do with it? It's never too late. One tiny step after another keeps moving you in the direction of your dream; it's the journey and the experience that matters most. No matter how long it takes, you're moving forward.

Taking action that aligns with your goals is critical. Keep one foot in reality to monitor and address concerns, but keep the other foot in your dreams and continue to think beyond the limitations of the reality you live in today.

"The secret to getting ahead is getting started."
—**Mark Twain**

Learn the Turtle Trick: break action steps down to small manageable steps, or turtle steps. So often we look way out into the future and get overwhelmed with the scope, the unknown, or how to create the final picture. It becomes too monstrous to approach or begin, so we shut down altogether and never get started. We don't have to have all the answers, have every step mapped out, or know exactly what it will look like in order to get started. The answers or next steps have a way of revealing themselves as you go along. It's about trusting the process if you just keep putting one foot in front of the other.

Start by having an end goal in mind by determining your desired outcome. But, know it will probably change and adjust as you move forward. Putting off getting started because you're caught up in the idea that you need the exact formula or need to know exactly what it will look like when it's complete is the biggest buzz kill! This perfectionism and can create immobilization; it keeps you stuck in reality and shuts down the dreamer. If you believe you need to have it all figured out to get started, throw out that belief now! This is probably the core reason why people never take action on a dream or goal. Make this your motto: "Don't make change too complicated; just begin."

"Don't make change too complicated; just begin."
—Unknown

Let's say you have a dream or goal. Maybe it is to start an online business for a very unique home décor design service. You have a talent for designing and creating accent furniture pieces that reflect the client's personality and tastes. You don't know exactly how to formulate the business or how you will make enough money at it, so you don't do anything to get started—even though it is your passion, people love your creations, and it excites you to think about doing it as a career. The trick is to keeping one foot in reality and one in your dream, and letting the idea develop and formulate as you go. But you also need to take a step today to begin taking you down *the yellow brick road.* Make a list of all the things you would need to get started. Examples for this particular dream might be photos of your work, a website, a Facebook page, and business cards. Create a list and a timeline to implement, while giving yourself permission to adjust as you go.

"Big things often have small beginnings."
—Unknown

Here is what no one may have ever told you: break down the actions into such small steps that you have no resistance to completing them. For example, you could say to yourself, "I am going to spend one hour, five days per week, creating my website." If that feels overwhelming or like too much, break it down to a half hour per day, fifteen minutes per day, or only three days per week. Keep making it smaller until you can say to yourself, "I can do that!" Try it on in your body. Close your eyes and think about the step and the commitment level. How does it feel in your body? Do you feel light and excited, or do you feel dread and it will be a stretch? Here's your very own unique body compass telling you if it works for you. Keep making the steps smaller until your goal feels manageable and effortless. A commitment of a teeny-tiny step three days per week is way more effective than never getting started at all because it feels overwhelming. Breaking life's actions and dreams down into turtle steps is so important—I cannot stress it enough. This behavior determines your ability to make your dream come true. You will be surprised how taking some small actions will inspire you; momentum can take over by just getting started. Maybe you said, "I'm going to spend fifteen minutes every day doing *xyz*." You sit down and before you know it, it's an hour later, because your passion took over.

Let go of thinking it must turn out or look a specific way. The magic gets lost when we become rigid with our expectations. Just by taking action, a dream can take on a life of its own. The dream can transcend into something even greater than you originally imagined when you open to possibilities and open to the flow of the universe. Let go of attachments and miracles can happen.

Sometimes we just don't know what we don't even know; be okay with that. You can always change course if needed. Nothing is permanent. We get caught up in thinking every decision we make is a major or permanent one, and we overthink it, take it too seriously, as if the decision we make will be locked in for life. This will create a fear of trying something new; it's playing small.

I have recently thought about moving somewhere new for the adventure. I have been in Tampa for more than twenty-five years now. My kids are grown; my daughter is living in New York City, and my son wants to join the military. I can do my job from anywhere. The only thing holding me in Tampa is the familiarity and a few close friends. Wondering "what if I don't like it there?" is keeping me from taking action. I have been viewing my choice as permanent.

If I don't like it, so what? It doesn't have to be forever, and I could always move back to Tampa. When I took the "permanent" factor out of my perspective, it opened up a feeling of freedom to explore the possibilities with excitement, not fear.

Trust and believe in YOU!

Step 3: Trust in the process.

If you are working from a foundation of purpose and passion, which lights you up when you think about making your dream a reality, then you can assure yourself your compass is pointing you to your true north. There is no way you can go wrong. The worst thing that can happen is you end up somewhere you hadn't thought of, because your heart is now your director and taking you to new heights. Trust knowing without seeing. Believe in the miraculous you for no other reason than that you are here. There is no way to go wrong when your heart is in charge of your being. Even if you fail, you will learn and grow to a level you have yet to experience. Allow yourself to be a beginner. No one starts off being excellent.

Building your dreams is not easy, or else everyone would do it. But taking your dreams through imagination into reality is simply about taking action.

Believing in yourself and knowing that you are worthy are the most precious gifts you could ever offer yourself. It takes practice. When you find yourself in doubt, cheer yourself on. I find myself discouraged at times with how things are going in starting my business, especially when I am not successful at something or things aren't moving along as I anticipated. It is really easy to go into, "Who am I to do this?" or "I am not capable, smart enough, or talented enough."

Catch yourself here quickly, before it drags you down the rabbit hole, and turn it around. Immediately say or write down three successes or three experiences you have had that show you are in fact so capable and the right person to create and achieve the dream.

Self-encouragement, self-endorsement, and perseverance are critical to any success worth having. Don't give up too soon. Think about this: *It's really hard to beat a person who never gives up.* If you feel in any way like maybe you're giving up too soon, then it's too soon. Either you succeed or it will morph into something else. Patience is keeping a great attitude while waiting for your dream to be realized. Patience is just another word for love and self-love. You have to do whatever it takes to continually reignite or realign with that place within that got you started on your dream in the first place. Find the things that will realign you with passion and enthusiasm as a regular practice, not just when you get discouraged or off-track. For me, those things have been interaction with like-minded people, support from other entrepreneurs, mastermind groups, and events or conferences that are about inspiration.

"The laws of success and failure are consistent."
—Unknown

Step 4: Declare your dream.
Dreams don't depend on your circumstance or history. A one-degree shift greatly changes the trajectory of where you end up after just six months. Think about a ship in the ocean changing its course by one degree; that boat will end up somewhere significantly different. So, don't ever underestimate how the smallest shift or action can change your life course and experience.

We are spiritual beings having a human experience. The mind that thinks it can, creates it in reality. What are you thinking about? Do you want to bring what you're thinking about into reality? Energy follows attention. Where are you putting your attention, and what are you putting it on? Bring your attention to what you want, not on what you don't want. For example, let's say you want to lose weight. Thinking and saying, "I don't want to be fat," is not going to get you any thinner. Your attention is on what you don't want—"being fat"— so you will create more "being fat." Consciously focus your thoughts and attention on what want. The spin would be "I am getting thinner every day" or "I am thin." You change the internal, not the external, circumstances. Learn to think from your dream or goals.

The key is to learn how to really pay attention to what you want to pay attention to:

- Notice your body, toes, head, and fingers.
- Notice what you have been thinking.
- Notice what you have been feeling: interested, bored, happy?

You have to notice in order to harness it. There is nothing good or bad in what you notice; it all depends on what you choose to notice. When you believe an experience is bad, wait three days to find some good in it. Ask yourself, "How could this circumstance work to my advantage?

You can schedule your own panic. You can choose how you will feel, instead of letting the condition have mastery over you. You choose to not dive into an initial emotional reaction by saying, "I will deal with it later." This will often negate the whole panic or upset. It only takes sixty seconds for an emotion to subside if you do not react or act out from the emotion. This simple practice could bring much needed peace to our homes, our roads, and our world.

These principles aren't magic. They're the operating system by which we live our lives. What we believe becomes true. You are the thermostat of your life. You decide how you want to set it and then determine what is needed or wanted to create your dreams.

❧

"Reception is the key to learning, but practice is the key to mastery."
—Unknown

Nothing that happens is pure luck or random. When you think, feel, and project clearly, life becomes more precise. When you are vague or constantly changing what you want, you get exactly that—nothing specific. The universe cannot deliver without clarity of what you put out there.

In realizing life or the world as energy, it becomes easy to understand how a single action or shift can be far-reaching and infinite. Just as you are one person, you are made up of five billion to 200 million trillion cells. Developing cancer is like a group of cells going rogue within your body and then eventually, if balance and health is not created, the cells will begin affecting the entire body. The planet or the universe is the same concept. Every living thing on the planet or within the universe is like one cell within your body. We are all one, not separate; everything and everyone is energetically connected. It is what I call God, the universal fabric, the divine spark that connects us all.

The light of the universe projects through us. We are all connected.

If we are all energetic subsystems of a greater system, the universe, then we are all light and it projects through us as invisible energy. The unique lens that we each view the world with determines what we see. Most of our perspectives are like viewing life through a kaleidoscope. Our minds are not clear; they are inundated with judgments and past experiences, projected from the thinking mind—not the clarity of our truth. Light that projects through clear glass remains pure light. Light that projects through various filters looks totally different. It is why each human being can see the exact same thing in the world in an entirely differently way.

We can all have a dark chapter in life, but that does not have to determine your whole book. You can have success or failure in any area of your life, but neither has to determine the future. During a particularly difficult pose in my yoga class, Ashley Halley, the teacher, said, "Yes, I know it sucks. SO WHAT?" That one statement alone could elevate so much of our suffering in life. Changing the lens or removing the filter causes us to see something as wrong or bad. Sometimes life situations are going to suck, but we don't have to make it mean anything about anything. We certainly don't have to let it become a dark cloud over everything else. Life can be sad, difficult, and challenging. It is just an experience and it will pass. It is only when we are in these uncomfortable places that we allow it to overshadow our lives, as if the sky is falling. Accepting discomfort and inviting it in, instead of fighting, hating, or resisting it, allows any experience to pass easier and quicker.

Step 5: Spend your time with people who energize you and support your dream.

The people we spend the most time with become the common denominator for who we are and how we behave and show up in the world. Looking at it in the extreme, if you want to become a highly evolved person who wants to make positive changes in the world, hanging out with drug addicts or gang members will not support you in rising upward. Now I know that sounds really silly, duh! But, if everything is energy, who we hang out with has a huge effect on vibration—even when those people are only slightly below where we want to be. Whoever is in our proximity the most will be the common denominator for determining at what level we think and behave. The company you keep is critical in determining your success.

Try this exercise:

1. Look at the seven people in your life you spend the most time with.
2. Write them down in a list.
3. Place a plus sign next to each person that is a positive and supportive influence in your life. In other words, you feel great around them, you enjoy being with them, they uplift and support you, and they give you energy.

4. Place a minus sign next to the people you spend time with that are difficult and take a lot of effort to be around. In other words, they bring you down; they can suck the life out of you.

If there were no minus signs on your list, you are way above average in ensuring you surround yourself with supportive people. Congratulations!

If you have one or more minus signs next to people in your life, I would bet these relationships are ones that feel obligatory. They are probably family members or someone that has been in your life a long time, possibly a spouse or long friendship.

Here is where you can start becoming conscious and fully aware of who you give yourself and your time to. It is critical for your own journey inward and upward to only give yourself to those that give fully back. If they don't feed you, it's time to take a look at drawing some healthy boundaries in those relationships. Remember, you have to be your biggest supporter and keeper of the gate of your energy. If they are family members, it may mean you learn to detach and love them from afar. It means that you choose how much time and energy you offer those relationships. If they only take from you and there is no return at all, detach and move on. Those people are like cancer to your spirit and self-worth. Think of a hot air balloon. The only way to rise up in the sky is to start dropping the sand bags. People in your life can be doing the same thing to you, holding you down. They can become weights that keep you from transcending to success, happiness, and your dreams.

Let go of feeling responsible for anyone else's journey in life. You are not God; it's arrogant for us to think we are responsible for another person's life or life experiences. That belief only keeps us from focusing on our own life, which we are totally responsible for. It's not your job to sacrifice yourself or allow yourself to suffer. Not only is this behavior counterproductive for your own life, it doesn't support or help the other person either. The most loving thing you can offer another is to be a role model for healthy boundaries and taking care of yourself first. Whether or not they choose to shift is not your business. You are your business. You are the one and only thing you can control during your life.

Let's say you are starting a new venture, getting married, getting divorced, or changing careers and your mother is not supportive and telling you all the reasons you shouldn't do it. You don't have to engage with her or have her approval; you only need your own approval. Her opinion is based on her experience and filters, along with her own fear. It doesn't mean she doesn't want the best for you. My own mother was notorious for telling me how I should decorate or how I should be raising my kids. To me, her unsolicited opinions came across as criticism and I would immediately become defensive. It created a lot of arguments and conflict in our relationship and it usually left me feeling like I was never good enough. This one response alone could have drastically changed the dynamics of our relationship: "Thanks for sharing your thoughts or feelings, but this works for me!" This one statement alone can save a lot of drama in our lives. It also requires letting go of needing someone's approval.

Step 6: Fly your freak flag!

"When in doubt, make a fool of yourself. There is a microscopically thin line between being brilliantly creative and acting like the most gigantic idiot on earth. So what the hell—leap."

—**Cynthia Heimel**

Flying your freak flag happens when you are ready to step into integrity with your soul's purpose. It is living from you authentic self. It's what makes you unique and letting that define you. You become essential in your own life by being in harmony with your own purpose. The worry of what anyone else thinks falls away, because you are so okay with whom you are and external approval is no longer sought after.

I was recently at an IT conference and they did a kick-off by asking a few random people to come on stage and speak spontaneously. Each participant was given a random slide and the topic was the shifting of the Earth's plate tectonics. The second participant was given a slide showing a photo of a middle-aged, slightly overweight man wearing a tutu in the middle of a cow pasture. At that moment, I wanted to speak about the slide so badly. I had a whole message about how flying our freak flags and being our essential self is the most healing thing we could do to save the core of the earth. I loved the photo because we all have that in us, but we are not all willing to be that vulnerable and silly.

Being vulnerable and silly is play in the purest form. I truly believe that when we are being goofy and letting ourselves spontaneously play, we are the most lovable. It's what makes us beautiful.

Step 7: Practice gratitude.

"The whole process of mental, spiritual, and material riches may be summed up in one word—gratitude."

—Joseph Murphy

The universe loves gratitude, and the more you find to be grateful for, the more the universe provides you with to be grateful. It is a form of magic. Putting attention on what you want more of will bring you more of what you want.

I encourage you to develop the habit of being grateful for absolutely everything in your life. This has many benefits including altering our mindset from one of lack, to one of privilege. This also changes other peoples' perceptions of us and good things suddenly start showing up in our lives with regular frequency.

My good friend Lisa from college reminded me a few months ago that when I am out and about in the world, I am so discerning of everything, that my body language makes me seem unapproachable and aloof. She said she knows that is not my true essence and she believes the whole world needs to see the Steimy (my nickname from college) that she has so much fun with. I took this to heart and tried it out in the world and the results were nothing shy of extraordinary the first time I did it.

I had a trip planned to Key West for a long weekend and was going to meet a friend and her brother at their condo. They had to cancel, but I decided to go by myself since I already had a non-refundable ticket. This was all about getting me out of my comfort zone. Sure enough, the day before I left, Cisco Systems gave me notice and a very abundant severance package. It turned out to be perfect timing for me to get out of town and into a whole new mindset. I went out by myself the first evening and put on a smiling face, opened my heart, and asked for whatever was in my highest good to show up. I met not one, but two wealthy men that night. One of them was entertaining clients for the weekend and I was invited along for the rest of the weekend to be wined and dined and go out on sunset yachting trips. As I was out on a lovely boat in the beautiful blue Caribbean in sunny eighty-degree weather, a wave of gratitude came over me that I cannot even begin to fully express in words. The more gratitude I give, the more abundance and beauty I receive in my life. It the most amazing thing! The universe loves gratitude, so the more you express gratitude, the more you receive life's riches.

In Brené Brown's research, she discovered one of the characteristics common among all people who lived life with their whole heart was that they had a gratitude practice.[12] Having or feeling gratitude and practicing gratitude are two very different things. After all, you can have yoga pants and wear them often, but that doesn't mean you have a yoga practice. If you only adopt one thing from this book, develop a gratitude practice. Gratitude is vitality for life. A gratitude practice allows you to feel joy when life is chaotic or difficult. This one simple practice can change your life significantly. To begin a gratitude practice, keep a gratitude journal and pick a certain time every day to use it. I recommend morning to set your tone for the day or at the end of each day as a reflection.

Write down or say aloud ten things you are grateful for from the day. It doesn't have to be big things, it can be little appreciations.

I alternate—sometimes I say mine out loud as I am walking home from my morning workout, or I write them in the journal next to my bed before I turn out the light.

Here are some sample gratitude expressions: I am grateful my legs can perform for me; I am grateful for my dog's company on my run; I am grateful for the beautiful sky; I am grateful for the cardinal I saw; I am grateful that my friend could meet me today to workout.

They can be big things too—your health, your income, your relationship, your children, and so on. Just express your gratitude. Get it out of your head and on paper or hear your own voice express gratitude. See what happens in your life. By focusing on what you appreciate, you literally create a life you appreciate.

You can sign up on my website for a free thirty-day gratitude practice, where you will receive an email from me every day for thirty days that will include a new gratitude practice for each day. Visit LisaMarieJenkins.com.

Step 8: Go within.

This is the most foundational practice for every decision when dealing with life's difficulties and finding your compass. Going inward before living outward is the recipe to live authentically! When we invest more energy in developing our internal spiritual lives, the outward begins to take care of itself.

Conclusion

The Gift

very relationship offers a gift, no matter how poorly it is wrapped. *New York Times* bestselling author Gregg Braden is world renowned for bridging science, ancient wisdom, and practical living. He calls relationships "our temples of initiation." Whether a relationship is momentary or for a lifetime, each one offers us an opportunity to learn, grow, and evolve. Whenever there is an emotional charge in a relationship, there's a lesson—the bigger the charge, the bigger the lesson. This is especially true with the romantic relationship; it can be your biggest temple of initiation to enlightenment.

As I look back at my significant romantic relationships and even the short-lived ones, they all provoked some level of suffering, and feelings of abandonment that brought my stuff to the surface. I now see each and every one of them as a beautiful soulful gift. Each offered me an opportunity to evolve and find passion and purpose from within. I am truly grateful for every experience, especially the ones that brought me to my knees.

As I think back to my three significant relationships—Bill, Greg, and Jeff—only gratitude prevails. Each were excruciating during their evolution, especially when they ended. Yet, I would not be the person I am today without them. It would be so easy to see myself as a victim and focus on how they were wrong and I was betrayed. There is no point; it is not about them—it's about me. I am genuinely in a place of total forgiveness and appreciation for our paths coming together. I forgive myself for all the times I was less than loving to them due my own fear and disparity. I see each and every one of them with compassion and love. I am also grateful they didn't last or work out; I would have not accelerated my growth had we married. There are so many things I would have never attempted, accomplished, or achieved had I stayed with any one of them.

After Bill, I went on to compete in three triathlons, and due to the pain I was experiencing, I was willing to try anything and began my inward journey through therapy and a spiritual quest. Bill used to always say to me, "I have never known anyone that cares more about bettering themselves than you." I think that is the greatest compliment he could have ever offered.

Greg gave me the ability to be alone, while knowing he was there. I knew he loved me, but a year in Iraq left me alone. I continued to pursue my spiritual life, began understanding spiritual laws, and found the strength to dig myself out of a hole that was so deep I couldn't see sunlight. I learned to rely on me and went on to do some amazing work in my corporate career. I also developed an amazing yoga practice, I went to yoga teacher training, and yoga still guides me today.

Jeff ended up being the icing on my cake in regards to transformation through the ring of fire. He is the reason I finally understood my relationship to thought and how I was the cause of my own suffering, not him or any guy. Through the ending of that relationship, I learned how to become present and in the moment. I developed a vigilant practice of being present, observing thought, and redirecting thought. I was driven to end my suffering. I finally began to value myself and no longer saw my self-worth as a reflection of a guy being with me or not. Could there be a greater gift from another soul?

Based on the story I've told thus far, you may be wondering—how did I get to this point? There was a point where everything magically came together for me, and I shifted my life drastically. I had been learning about the power of thought (the thinking mind) and how to be present for a while, but mostly at an intellectual level. Actually putting this intellectual knowledge into practice over time, and being vigilant about observing my thoughts and shifting them, is a whole different ballgame. This major shift happened after some time of practicing being present—in other words, *devotion*. Interesting how the word "devotion" is used in so many religions, yet it has come to be associated with outward practices. It is rarely associated with the inward experience of being present, which is how we become fully connected to God or spirit. It is ultimately how we end all suffering and truly enter the kingdom of heaven. What I learned is that the left brain thinks about what it is used to, not what is good for you. I was finally able to embody this concept at age forty-four, after my breakup with Jeff.

I had met Jeff about eight months after my breakup with Greg, the Blackhawk pilot. I was not completely healed and was still desperately seeking a relationship to replace him. My physical attraction to Jeff was overwhelming. I am sure this was due to the mindfuck that became the rhythm of our relationship. He would emotionally pull me in, and then the moment we truly connected, he would push me away. It felt something like this: come here, go away, come here, go away. I knew he was capable of emotionally connecting at a deeper level (the hook), but his emotional withdrawal after every deep, loving connection devastated me. Talk about bringing up my wounded little kid! Of course, the minute I would let go of him and end the relationship, his own scared and wounded child would jump back in full force, and I would allow myself to give it another round, only to repeat the same painful cycle over again.

An entire year after the relationship finally ended, I had still not emotionally let go. One major reason was that he would keep reaching out just to make sure I was still there and still responding, and I bought it hook, line, and sinker. But I had finally reached the point where my suffering was so great, I was willing to do whatever it took to escape the suffering once and for all. This relationship would be my last relapse before I finally became clean from my relationship addiction.

I had also just started a spiritual book club with my friend Julie. She had introduced me to the concept of "my thoughts are killing me." My thoughts were literally making me miserable, but at the time I thought my suffering was all Jeff's fault. Nope—it was my habitual "stinkin' thinkin'" about him. A few months into the book club, Julie recommended we read *My Stroke of Insight* by Jill Bolte Taylor. Jill was a brain researcher with a PhD from Harvard and a very dominant left brain personality. One morning, when Jill was in her mid-thirties, she was at home getting ready to go to work and had a stroke in the left hemisphere of her brain. In the midst of her experience, she was able to observe her left brain go on and off line from a scientific point of view. As the hemorrhage became more severe, the left brain began to shut down, and her right brain completely took charge, she describes her experience as one that only mystics have shared. She felt nirvana, a peacefulness, and saw everything as energy.

After her stroke, Jill had to learn to do everything over again, just like an infant. Her left-brain data files were completely gone. It took her seven years to fully recover, with the exception of fully recovering her math skills. Since then, she has become an advocate for helping people understand the care stroke victims really need, and teaches on the importance of balancing left-brain and right-brain thinking. Her book did a wonderful job of explaining the relationship between the hemispheres in detail, and advises us that our path to peace lies in our ability to make sure our left brain does not become our master.

Ultimately, her book is responsible for the epiphany that changed the course of my life. Not only did it bring an end to my suffering from the break-up with Jeff, it put an end to any severe suffering for the rest of my life thus far. At that point, I had previously read many books about the relationship between suffering and thought, such as Byron Katie's *Loving What Is*. I had fully understood them and they had resonated with me, but I was unable to embody the lesson and make the shift in my life. Sometimes I wonder whether we just need to hear something a certain way before the "Aha" moment happens, or whether it is the accumulation of hearing the same thing said in different ways that finally leads us to the kind of understanding that allows us to actually apply it and practice it. Either way, it is a journey that takes time, and we all get it when we get it and not a moment sooner.

For whatever reason, when I read Jill's book, I finally understood that the more often we think something and the longer we think it, those thought patterns become hardwired in the left hemisphere, much like ruts or carved-out channels imprinted in our brain. The visual in Jill's book helped me understand this in a way I never had before. Remember, the brain doesn't think what is good for you; it thinks what it is used to thinking. Our habitual thoughts run our lives if we are completely unaware of what we are thinking— in other words, asleep!

I finally realized my suffering had nothing to do with what Jeff was or wasn't doing. In fact, it had nothing to do with Jeff at all. It was a major tipping point in my life, because now I could take responsibility for my experience and had the power to make a change. Because I had habitually kept thinking the same negative thoughts over and over again about Jeff, I had created a pattern, or deep rut, in my brain. That meant that my suffering was caused purely by habitual thinking—nothing more. Of course, simply thinking new thoughts isn't easy. The longer we think particular thoughts or thought patterns, the harder it is to even realize what you are thinking. These thoughts become hardwired and triggers become subconscious.

Here began the devotion I referred to earlier—my vigilant practice of observing my thoughts. How did I do it? I created my own particular visual technique; every time a thought about Jeff entered my awareness, I would immediately visualize this thought as a dark pattern in my left brain. Then I would quickly visualize the most beautiful radiant light dissipating or dissolving that dark pattern. This practice was not easy; as I said, it took great vigilance and conscious effort. I had to stay on top of it and be fully present. But it is also what "waking up" is all about—being fully checked in to what we are thinking and redirecting ourselves.

In the first week, I was probably doing this literally a thousand times per day, but with each day, the thoughts came up less and less often. Remember, I had habitually been thinking about Jeff and associating him with my lack of wellbeing and peace for over a year now. This pattern was deeply embedded in my brain. Within a month, I had completely released the thought pattern. It was amazing. I now knew how to relieve suffering from my mind. I was free! I now know I have the skill to make sure I never suffer that way again, in any situation in life. This practice of devotion strengthened my consciousness so that it could be fully present in any situation. Also, I believe my particular technique worked well for me because I am a visual person. I could see my thoughts visually, which allowed me to more intuitively understand my mind's relationship to thoughts in the moment, so I could literally see each thought and therefore change it.

By the way, although I have a deep knowing that I will never have to suffer again, that doesn't mean I don't have feelings or emotions any longer. I still feel grief or sadness; those are natural and necessary to be healthy. However, suffering is totally optional and unnecessary. Emotions are a choice, not a reaction, and we can only be equipped to make a choice when we can identify the soundtrack of our minds.

The soundtrack in our minds includes the stories we tell ourselves about ourselves and the stories we tell ourselves about what an experience really means. This soundtrack determines the way we feel—not external circumstances or the experience itself. It is the lens through which we view and experience the world.

What is the soundtrack playing in your head? If you know your soundtrack has created ruts in your left brain that are hurting you rather than helping you, take a moment right now and try the visual technique I described above. If you can't identify a thought immediately, you can always start with the way you feel. Catch yourself quickly when you are feeling lousy—whether you're sad, upset, or depressed, or feel a knot in your stomach or throat. Also, if you're more of a verbal person than a visual person, you can also shift your thoughts by stating positive, affirming statements. Even if the affirming statements feel untrue or you feel silly at first, do it anyway. "Acting as if" has always propelled me forward in life, and it can work for you as well. I have always overstepped what I thought I might be ready for, believing I could do it—and I always succeeded. Try saying positive affirmations out loud in a mirror. No matter how silly you feel, do it! The results speak for themselves. Research has shown that looking into our own eyes and hearing our own voice is amazingly effective in helping us believe in ourselves and create change. Changing your head's soundtrack in these ways – or whatever technique works for you - will allow you to go from fear to love and from pain to compassion, simply by becoming curious and observing your thoughts.

Although the end of my relationship with Jeff provided the most profound healing, each of my relationships was a significant milestone or temple of initiation in finding my way home, to me, to my soul. My greatest suffering happened in these relationships, yet they each contributed to my journey of finding self-love and self-worth. I am awake and now know that I am the one I had always been waiting for. I am beautiful, whole, and home. The next relationship will be based in joy, ease, and wholeness with a spiritual foundation. I know this, because I committed to not settling.

My friend Ashley uses the word MOVE as an acronym, and I love it—Me On a Victorious Evolution! I think it applies perfectly to us as women when it comes to moving on from a romantic relationship that has reached its end. So many of us believe that when we end a relationship, we need to explain everything to our partner in agonizing and nauseating detail, with justification to boot. But all we have to share is: "This isn't going to work for me." We can remember the gift inherent in every relationship. We don't have to justify to anyone why something isn't in alignment with our highest good and why we are choosing to honor ourselves. We only have to MOVE!

So the suffering I experienced in romantic relationships was the greatest gift I ever received. It allowed me to learn the true path of peace and presence, which I may have never had the desire to learn if I hadn't been in so much pain. I also believe the same is true for you. Whatever has brought you your greatest pain is your path home and your salvation. Whatever you have spent thousands and thousands of hours on trying to fix, analyze, control, or think your way out of is your path home to your greatness and your true inner light.

Unfortunately, suffering is what usually propels us to embark on the journey of devotion. It is still a gift.

Remember, *you* have a message and gift to share that is as unique to you as your fingerprint. When you feel free to MOVE, in alignment with your true nature and living the truth of who you are, you are not only fulfilling your purpose, you are fulfilling your responsibility to contribute to the healing of the world through your feminine leadership.

Your answers, passion, and purpose are within you and accessible to you in every moment. Welcome home, Beauty! You are the one you have always been waiting for!

Your 12 Steps to Waking Up
and Coming Home to Yourself

1. Believe in yourself.
2. Learn to be happy alone, to enjoy your own company.
3. It's always about you, not the outer circumstances or anyone else.
4. Take action, no matter how small the step towards your dreams.
5. Let go of needing external approval.
6. Stop living your life by what others think.
7. Choose discomfort over resentment.
8. Feel the fear and saddle up anyway.
9. Practice gratitude.
10. Live with your whole heart.
11. Emerge. Align. Evolve.
12. Be fully present: Live it, share it, KICK ASS!

Appendix

My Legacy

Like all of us, my journey began well before I was born, affected by events I never witnessed but were part of my inheritance. The most profound part of my legacy was my mother's incredible story. Over the years, I have shared my mother's upbringing and life with others and the common response was usually, "You need to write a book!" Documenting my family's history was my original intent when I started writing, and then the book took on a life of its own. But it really all comes down to the same story. Even though I had achieved the American dream in many ways, with a successful six-figure career in the technology industry thousands of miles from where my mother grew up, her legacy still lived on inside me. And I would have to face it. In tribute to my mother and the treasures her legacy has left me, not the least of which was the writing of this book, I'd like to include a more complete version of her story here.

My mother, Helen Ruth Thorpe, was born on March 14, 1926, on a rural family farm in Licking, Missouri. She began working as a field hand at age seven. Her mother, Florence Jackson, had been married off (sold off) at age fifteen to Aca Thorpe. He was twice her age with three young children she would now be responsible for. Florence had four more children with Aca; my mother was her third child and the youngest girl.

The Thorpe family was poor, ignorant, worked to the bone, and faced plenty of beatings with a switch. Although I never knew Aca, I heard that he was quite the drunk, which added to his physical abuse. The kids were told they were "good for nothing" if they weren't "being useful and working." My mother's upbringing is a very real story of walking miles to school in the snow, one pair of shoes a year, and no medical care. In fact—brace yourself here—my mother told me that when she was growing up, she would often pick up tapeworms from the farm animals and that it was not uncommon for her to find a foot-long tape worm in her stool. The home treatment: a nice big spoonful of kerosene with a little sugar added to help it go down. Well, at least they tried to make it taste good! This was probably the cause of my mom's digestive issues throughout her life.

To say she had a difficult upbringing is an understatement. When my mom was thirteen and started her menstrual cycle, she had no idea this would happen to her one day. She actually thought the bleeding meant she must be dying. As a response, her mother threw some rags to her and told her to use them until the bleeding stopped. One of my mother's jobs as a child was to empty the pee pots each morning into the outhouse. She recalled, on more than one occasion, that there was a tiny fetus in her mother's pot. These were apparently my grandmother's miscarriages, but it's shocking to know that an innocent young girl was exposed to it with no explanation. Many other things would make you cringe; let your imagination run wild and you will probably be spot-on with whatever you come up with.

The first and only time my mom saw a doctor while living with her parents was after her sister had accidentally dropped a load of firewood on her hand. The wood severed the end of her finger. It was crudely reattached, and she ended up with a deformed finger and no fingernail. I'm sure the only reason this particular incident received medical attention was because it meant she may not be able to work on the farm.

Aca and Florence divorced long before I was born. My mother told me that she attended Aca's funeral and it felt like a cloud of dark evil lifted when he passed. She truly didn't have a kind thought or word about him; by all accounts he was a loveless and cruel father.

My mother was the only one of seven siblings to graduate from high school. They were encouraged to quit school after 8th grade so they could work on the farm full-time. At seventeen, my mom promptly took her diploma and

Helen Ruth Thorpe (left front) and family, 1931.

moved to St. Louis, Missouri. She told me many stories of sharing apartments with other girls and working in factories, even as a welder during WWII.

Her first date in St. Louis was with a man that took her out for pizza. She had never had pizza before and vividly recounted biting into the bubbly hot cheese and burning the roof of her mouth. She was so embarrassed that she didn't know any better that she did her best not to react, trying to play it cool to avoid looking like a county hick.

My mother made a conscious decision to learn social graces, manners, and proper societal etiquette. She was self-taught and an avid reader. Nothing about her indicated she had come from such a horrific and crude upbringing. She had could carry on a conversation about any topic and appeared quite sophisticated. I remember her setting the most formal holiday dinner tables, with silver, crystal, and china.

Helen Ruth Thorpe, high school graduation, 1943.

The dinner rules were very clear —shirt must be worn, hats must be off, and no cans or bottles on the table.

She met my father, Edward Roy Steinmeyer, when she was twenty-three. She was four days older than him but let him believe he was a year older until after the marriage was official. It's so funny to me that she had a problem being the "older woman" by four days. Somehow she thought that would not be acceptable to my father or society.

My father was a gentle giant, but a real guy's guy. He had a sensitive soul. His German upbringing taught him to hold all emotion inside. I believe this is ultimately why he had a heart attack and died at the young age of forty-six. He was the neighborhood hero—tall, lean, easygoing, friendly, athletic, social, and well-liked by friends and relatives. He enjoyed simplicity in life: a barbeque with the neighbors, golfing with his best friend, or a Cardinals baseball game. Though not particularly ambitious, he was a committed man, a civil service kind of guy. He came from a long family lineage of civil service and military officers. He was the youngest of four children, three boys and a girl. His family was full of well-educated over-achievers—military officers and Wall Street financial millionaires; his sister was even a Navy officer and an Olympic diver.

**Ruth Steinmeyer,
1949 Marine Base pool,
Quantico, Virginia.**

My grandfather, Roy Von Steinmeyer was St. Louis' fire chief. They dropped the "Von" from "Steinmeyer" when they came from Germany to the United States, because they thought it was too long of a name. This has always disappointed me; being known as Lisa Marie Von Steinmeyer sounds very regal to me and represents a line of German bluebloods. Because of his upbringing, Dad did not know how to grieve when his best friend and police partner, Will Downing, was shot and killed while they were on the scene of a robbery. My dad also took gunfire during the shootout that grazed his head—then he was dragged behind the assailant's getaway car. This was a serious traumatic event that he never addressed emotionally, personally, or professionally. My mom told me he started drinking heavily after losing his partner, as I am sure it was the only way he knew to suppress the overwhelming feelings of grief.

A few months after my dad's partner passed, he finally broke down and cried in front of my mom. After twenty-three years of marriage and four kids, it was the first time she had seen him cry. He then asked her if she thought he was less of a man for crying. It hurts my heart to know that he needed to ask this.

My parents had three children, all less than two years apart. My mother always said "three in diapers under age four was a stressful life." I was born much later, as a surprise. My siblings were ten, twelve, and fourteen years old when I was born. At this point in my parents' life, they were struggling financially. My father was not a disciplinarian—he could not say "no" to us. My mother, on the other hand, had a heavy hand and spanked my older siblings on a regular basis. But, she was also an amazing caretaker when we were sick or emotionally hurting. She was compassionate and would have felt the pain for us herself if possible. I think that can only come from a truly empathetic mother. When I was a child and I got sick, my mother would put a little dinner bell on my night table so I could ring her whenever I needed something. I never asked her, but my guess is that she received extra concern or affection from her mother when she was sick as a young child, so she knew how to give it to us.

My brother Gordon got the worst of my mother's rage, due to being the oldest and the only boy. But my sisters received their share, too. My brother told me he could remember being spanked as a child and having no idea why or what he had done wrong. My sister Paula, the baby for ten years before I booted her from the throne (I'm not sure she has

My parents and siblings Gordon, Marsha, Paula, and me.

forgiven me yet!), told me that our mother would often yell up the stairs in warning for her and my oldest sister Marsha to be quiet and go to sleep. They were just kids; they shared a room and would giggle and carry on well past their bedtime. Paula said as soon as she heard Mom's feet hit the stairs, she would start crying—but Marsha never ever once shed a tear, no matter how bad the spanking got.

Much later in her life, my mother told me she would go to bed at night and pray to God to please not let her beat those kids again. She often wondered why our father never stepped in and tried to control her or hold her back. People sometimes don't know or are unaware of what they are doing when their own emotional pain and trauma is triggered. I know the sweetness and integrity my mom had; I know she truly loved us and wanted the best for all of us.

I have often wondered why I escaped the physical trauma my siblings experienced. Perhaps it is because I was a different generation, a different financial upbringing, and was raised without our biological father, because my dad had a heart attack and died when I was eight.

My mother really blossomed after my father's death. I know now that had he not died, her growth and spiritual discovery probably wouldn't have happened—therefore, she was more tempered raising me than my siblings. Maybe it was because she was older and wiser, and only had me to deal with instead of four kids. Or maybe she was just tired. She also began making a decent income by selling residential real estate. I am sure all these things contributed to why I was raised quite differently than my siblings.

After my father's death, she began a spiritual journey and developed her psychic abilities. She would do

Edward R. Steinmeyer dies; heroic U. City policeman

Funeral For E. R. Steinmeyer

Funeral services for acting Sgt. Edward R. Steinmeyer of the University City Police Department, who died of a heart ailment Monday night, will be at 10 a.m. tomorrow at the Schrader undertaking establishment, 500 Manchester Road, Ballwin.

Sgt. Steinmeyer was the officer who was with Patrolman Wilbert J. Downey when Downey was killed in attempting to stop a service station holdup Dec. 12, 1968. Sgt. Steinmeyer emptied his service revolver, wounding one of two robbers in an exchange of fire.

For his bravery he was given a Medal of Valor award by the Chamber of Commerce of Metropolitan St. Louis Sept. 9, 1970.

He became ill Christmas Eve at his home in 309 Buff Court, Ballwin, and was taken to St. John's Mercy Hospital, where he died. He was 45 years old.

Surviving are his wife, Helen, a son, Gordon, and three daughters, Marsha, Paula, and Lisa.

Edward R. Steinmeyer
Policeman dead

readings for people where she would hold onto a piece of their jewelry and meditate for a few minutes, then she would get a flood of images of people and situations—past, present, and future. She allowed the client to ask any questions they wanted. Afterwards, there would usually be a discussion in which my mom gave life advice or counseled them on how to take better care of themself. The more of a stranger you were to her, the more accurate her readings. She was a teacher and a healer—the real deal. She truly wanted to help and guide people.

I feel it is my legacy and true purpose in life to support and teach other women to live the truth of who they are. My mother died when I was thirty-nine years old. I had already started my spiritual quest. I know she would be proud of me today and that she is nodding in agreement that I am on the right path for this lifetime.

My mother gave me a wonderful spiritual foundation to build on, which left me open to less conventional thinking. She set the stage and I have now taken my spiritual healing and growth to the next level. I invite you, if you haven't already, to take a deeper look at your own legacy, particular the story of your mother. May it offer you insights to a quicker and easier path in finding clarity, freedom, peace, and passion.

Acknowledgments

This book became a reality due to all the people who said "cool" when I said I wanted to write a book. My inspiration started with people telling me I needed to write a book about my mother's life, a vision board that forced me to own my dream, and then an Author 101 University conference in 2013, in Los Angeles, which truly brought my writing into fruition.

I have immense gratitude for my teachers who brought me to my knees: Bill Rutherford, Greg McDonald, and Jeff Hilmer. They led me to my yellow brick road of spiritual awakening.

My therapists and spiritual teachers, Patricia Noll, Jill McCann, and Erina Cowan, brought guidance and direction to my life when I felt alone and confused. I could never have written this book without the insight and wisdom I learned from each of them.

I owe a huge thank you to yoga, and to the many special yoga teachers I have met over the last nine years—especially Ashley Halley, who taught me how to be more present, to lighten up, and to see everything as simply an experience without judgment.

Thank you to my dear friend and neighbor Anne, who always listened and always provided honest feedback along the way.

The authors who have had a profound effect on my life are Marianne Williamson, Byron Katie, Jill Bolte Taylor, and Martha Beck. I am grateful. It is amazing how the written word from someone else's experiences can change lives. I can only hope that my words will also help change lives, as your words have changed mine.

I am so appreciative of my editor, Amanda Rooker. Her talent and enthusiasm brought this book to life.

Finally, and most importantly, I am grateful to my mother and father for leaving me a legacy to heal, so I could serve the world with my message.

About the Author

Lisa Marie Jenkins is a professional speaker, author, and founder of Lisa Marie Jenkins, LLC—a consulting company specializing in igniting change in the world through feminine leadership.

Previously, Lisa spent more than twenty years in the technology industry at Cisco and Xerox in senior sales and marketing roles. During her Fortune 500 career, she realized that passion, connection, and purpose were often missing or hard to find in corporate life. She believes re-humanizing the workplace is necessary in order to drive true innovation, and the bottom line needs to include not only profit, but also the desire to serve the greater good.

Learn more or connect at LisaMarieJenkins.com.

Endnotes

1 Brené Brown, *Daring Greatly: How the Courage to Be Vulnerable Transforms the Way We Live, Love, Parent, and Lead* (Gotham, 2012).

2 Tiffani Lennon, "Benchmarking Women's Leadership in the United States," Colorado Women's College at the University of Denver, 2013, http://www.womenscollege.du.edu/media/documents/ BenchmarkingWomensLeadershipintheUS.pdf.

3 Nicholas D. Kristof, "Twitter, Women, and Power," *International New York Times*, Friday, October 25, 2013.

4 Ibid.

5 John Gerzema, "'Feminine' Values Can Give Tomorrow's Leaders an Edge," HBR Blog Network, August 12, 2013, http://blogs.hbr.org/2013/08/ research-male-leaders-should-think-more-like-women/.

6 Herminia Ibarra and Otilia Obodaru, "Women and the Vision Thing," Insead Global Leadership Centre's Study of the Top 10 Critical Components of Global Leadership, HBR.org, January 2009.

7 I learned this exercise from the Martha Beck Life Coach Training.

8 Brené Brown, *Daring Greatly: How the Courage to Be Vulnerable Transforms the Way We Live, Love, Parent, and Lead* (Gotham, 2012).

9   Sara H. Konrath, Edward H. O'Brien, and Courtney Hsing, "Changes in Dispositional Empathy in American College Students over Time: A Meta-Analysis," *Personality and Social Psychology Review* 15, no. 2 (May 2011): 180–198, http://psr.sagepub.com/content/15/2/180.short.

10 The practice of creating *mandalas* (Sanskrit for "circle" or "completion") has a long history and is a type of art therapy that has been proven to offer healing and can reveal amazing messages from our own spirit. The symbols and shapes of your mandala can represent a snapshot of your unconscious self. If you are interested in learning more or playing with art, I highly recommend Judith Cornell's *The Mandala Healing Kit* (SoundsTrue, 2006).

11 For more on this research, see http://completewellbeing.com/article/yoga-after-heart-surgery/, http://www.exaltedwarrior.com/, and http://www.yogawarriors.com/research.

12 Brené Brown, *Daring Greatly: How the Courage to Be Vulnerable Transforms the Way We Live, Love, Parent, and Lead* (Gotham, 2012).

CPSIA information can be obtained
at www.ICGtesting.com
Printed in the USA
FSOW01n0614190615
8102FS

9 781630 472436